A Life-Cycle Approach to Treating Couples

A Life-Cycle Approach to Treating Couples

From Dating to Death

Anne K. Fishel

MP **MOMENTUM** PRESS
HEALTH

MOMENTUM PRESS, LLC, NEW YORK

A Life-Cycle Approach to Treating Couples: From Dating to Death

First published in 2018 by
Momentum Press, LLC
222 East 46th Street, New York, NY 10017
www.momentumpress.net

ISBN-13: 978-1-94664-614-9 (paperback)
ISBN-13: 978-1-94664-615-6 (e-book)

Momentum Press Psychology Collection

Cover and interior design by Exeter Premedia Services Private Ltd., Chennai, India

First edition: 2018

10 9 8 7 6 5 4 3 2 1

Printed in the United States of America.

Abstract

Every couple can be located on a developmental time line, from first dates to final good-byes, and compared to the millions of other couples who have faced similar developmental challenges. Clinical knowledge about life-cycle stages serves as a reference point for the couple therapist, much as diagnoses do for the individual therapist.

Based on 30 years of couple therapy experience, Dr. Fishel, a Harvard Medical School professor, offers a practical guide for therapists at any stage of their own professional development. The author includes case examples and research findings about clients diverse not only in sexual orientation, but also age, race, ethnicity, class, and health.

The book focuses on the six major life-cycle changes that couples typically traverse, from dating to death.

- Stage one is about dating, partner selection, and the decision to make a long-term commitment.
- Stage two focuses on the couple's transformation during the transition to parenthood.
- Stage three is about midlife couples when there are increased work and parenting demands as well as care-giving of aging parents.
- Stage four is about late midlife couples who may be launching children, heading for retirement, and becoming grandparents.
- Stage five focuses on late-life couples, facing issues of aging, mutual dependency, and generational role changes.
- Stage six is about death as an endpoint to marriage, with a focus on illness, legacy, and saying good-bye.

For each stage, the author shares scientific research, common presentations and rich case examples, followed by developmentally-informed questions and topics for couple therapists to pursue.

Keywords

cohabitation, conflict, couple therapy, couples at end of life, couples in later life, couples at midlife, death, divorce, empty nest, family of origin, gay couples, gender differences, grandparents, illness, late midlife couples, launching children, lesbian couples, LGBTQ couples, life-cycle transitions, life-cycle, loss, marriage, midlife couples, parenting, post-retirement, retirement, same-sex couples, sexual functioning, sexual intimacy, sexuality, stages of development, transition to parenthood

Advance Praise for
A Life-Cycle Approach to Treating Couples

A seamless integration of elegant theory with in-the-office pragmatism, Dr. Fishel's graceful prose accomplishes the impossible task of making a text all things to all practitioners. Her comprehensive synthesis of the field's evidence into developmental stages, combined with a diligent anticipation of diversity among individuals and circumstances maintain the high utility that has defined all of Dr. Fishel's writings. The work is a most convenient framework for inquiry and intervention, giving as much attention to the *when* of relationships as to the *who* that comprise them.

—David Rubin, MD, Director,
Massachusetts General Hospital Psychiatry Academy;
Director of MGH Child and Adolescent Psychiatry
Residency Program

In her beautifully written portrait of the life cycle of couples, Anne Fishel has woven together research, memorable examples from her clinical practice and helpful suggestions for practitioners into a truly helpful guide. I was particularly impressed by her ability to approach couples in an accepting, nonpathologizing way. Any family therapist who reads this book will find him or herself better equipped to meet and help couples of any age on their marital journey.

—Michael Thompson, PhD,
co-author of *Raising Cain*

Anne Fishel has provided us with a rich, comprehensive, and evocative look at therapy for couples at different stages of the life cycle. She uses what is known from research and from vivid vignettes to provide helpful questions for therapists to pose to partners at each stage of life that will enrich their conversations and connections with one another. This volume will be invaluable for psychologists, psychiatrists, social workers, and those who train professional therapists to work with couples. I daresay it would also be eye-opening and helpful to couples themselves, who will surely find themselves in many of its rich examples.

—Carolyn Pape Cowan, PhD, Adjunct Professor of Psychology Emerita, University of California, Berkeley; Coauthor of *When Partners Become Parents: The Big Life Change for Couples*

In this exceptional book, Fishel draws on her years of experience and accumulated wisdom to produce an informative, reassuring, and practical reference that should be on the desk of every couple therapist. Organized logically and sequentially within a normalizing developmental framework, each of the carefully crafted chapters provides useful contextual information, vivid case examples, clinical strategies, some great questions to ask in session, and additional resources for understanding and intervening with distressed couples. This sensitive and timely text includes information for treatment with clients diverse not only in sexual identity, but also age, race, ethnicity, SES, health, and physical ability. Psychotherapists of all persuasions and all degrees of experience will find this a fascinating and welcome addition to the literature on working with couples.

—Martha B. Straus, PhD, Professor of Clinical Psychology, Antioch University New England, and author of *Treating Trauma in Adolescents: Development, Attachment, and the Therapeutic Relationship*

With this book, Anne Fishel has contributed a major advance to our understanding of couples and the practice of couple therapy. Her lifecycle perspective places the clinical at the center of the couple's world, and her many compelling case examples and relevant questions offer pragmatic help for navigating the challenging terrain of couples therapy. This is a book that complements the work of all couples therapists regardless of their preferred models.

—Douglas C. Breunlin
Program Director, Master of Science in Marriage and Family Therapy
Clinical Professor, Department of Psychology, Northwestern University

Contents

Acknowledgments

My heartfelt thanks to friends and colleagues at Massachusetts General Hospital who have supported my teaching and enhanced my understanding of couples' relationships over many years. In particular, I am grateful to the members of the decades-long MGH Reflecting Team, where I have spent hundreds of hours discussing couple therapy and learning from a very knowledgeable and generous team: Carol McSheffrey, LICSW; David Rubin, MD; Ellen Godena, LICSW; Pat Giulino, LICSW; Ginny Sigel, LICSW; Marie Herbert, LICSW; Nicole Simi, PhD; Julia Coleman, MD; Cindy Moore, PhD; Juliana Chen, MD; Shiri Cohen, PhD; Lisa Montanye, LICSW; and Abby McDonald, LICSW.

I am also very grateful to those clinicians who allowed me to interview them about their particular areas of expertise and who also provided perspectives on the manuscript: Bob Waldinger, MD, shared his knowledge about late-life couples, based on men and women who participated in the Harvard Study of Adult Development, which he directs; Paula Rauch, MD, and Cindy Moore, PhD, offered their deep stores of clinical experience about end-of-life-issues, based largely on their work at MGH's Parenting At a Challenging Time program, which Dr. Rauch founded and directs, and where Dr. Moore is the Associate Director; Leah Rosenberg, MD, a palliative care and hospice specialist at MGH, shared her wisdom about easing patients' suffering at end of life; Caroline Marvin, PhD, and Larry Rosenberg, PhD, senior clinicians in private practice with decades of couple therapy experience, talked with me about their work with same-sex couples. Eva Schoenfeld, PhD, Chris McElroy, PhD, Nancy Bridges, LICSW, Beth Harrington, PhD, Sue Wolff, MD, and Corky Becker, PhD have offered invaluable insights about couple work.

Several other therapists offered essential feedback on various chapters of this book. I am so appreciative of the thoughtful and incisive comments from Juliana Chen, MD; Melinda Morrill, PhD; Laura Prager, MD; and Abigail Judge, PhD.

Special thanks to three people who helped me track down articles during a wide-ranging literature search. Martha Stone, MS, the librarian at MGH's Treadwell Library, and my research assistants, Cara Lucke and Shay Haregnesh, went over and beyond in their efforts to find articles for this book.

I am very appreciative of initial feedback from Corinne Datchi, PhD, about the scope and focus of the book. I felt honored to have my former student, and now esteemed colleague, Anthony Chambers, PhD, offer a close reading of the entire book. He has certainly made the prose flow more smoothly and has greatly improved the content of the book.

I am very grateful to the hundreds of couples whom I have had the privilege to work with and learn from. If I know anything about the life cycle, it is from witnessing your lives.

Most of all, I want to thank my husband, Chris Daly, who is always my first and most trusted reader. He is unstinting in his encouragement and gentle with his criticism. Together we have traversed much of the life cycle together, from dating to the launching of our two adult sons. Although I know that there are special times in the stages that lie ahead, I'd really like to go back and relive all the stages again with him. To para-phrase the French writer Andre Maurois—a happy marriage is a long conversation that you wish would never end.

CHAPTER 1

Applying the Life-cycle Perspective to Couple Therapy

To everything there is a season, and a time to every purpose, under heaven.

—The Book of Ecclesiastes

If I were young again, I'd pay attention to that little-known dimension
A taste of endless time.
Just like water—it runs right through our fingers,
But the flavor of it lingers—Like a rich, red wine.

—Chris Smithers, *Leave the light on*

As therapists, we hear an abundance of stories, information, and anguish shared by couples during an initial evaluation and even more so, in therapy. This outpouring of data is a challenge for couple therapists to organize and render into a coherent framework for treatment. A life-cycle perspective locates every couple on a developmental timeline that starts with courtship and ends at death, divorce, or a relationship break-up, and offers context and a compass for what may feel like a confusing and cluttered landscape. Once the stage of development has been identified, a particular couple can be compared to the millions of other couples who have faced similar challenges at that same stage of development. Couple therapists, guided by the research on different life-cycle stages, can find their footing as they explore the challenges of a particular couple.

The couple's clinician can use the research on each stage of development in much the same way that the clinician trained in individual therapy uses research on diagnostic disorders. If, for example, an individual patient complains of low energy and a sad mood, a clinician will bring to bear all that is known about depression and ask questions accordingly—about feelings of worthlessness and guilt, disturbances in sleep and appetite, and difficulty concentrating. Most likely, every individual experiencing depression will not respond affirmatively to all of these queries, but the panel of questions will direct the therapist to explore a wide swath of experiences common among depressed individuals.

A couple therapist, with a focus on relationships rather than on individuals, does not rely on diagnostic categories like depression or anxiety. Instead, the couple therapist will compare a couple who presents at a particular stage of development with large groups of other couples who have been studied at that same stage. So, for example, when interviewing a couple with an infant, a couple therapist will ask about increases in fighting and decreases in sexual activity, as these behaviors have been identified as common features of thousands of couples making the transition to parenthood. A particular couple with a newborn may not endorse all the same experiences found in studies, but questions, rooted in research, will help orient the therapist to ask about a baby's temperament, sleep, and eating behavior, as well as to normalize disruptions in the couple's relationship. These questions can offer respectful, normative explanations of a couple's challenges. For example, "Most couples experience a decline in their sexual relationship in the first two years after becoming parents. How has this adjustment gone for you?" If a couple responds that they have transcended the normative expectations of this transition by avoiding fights about who is doing what and are having frequent and satisfying sex, it is an opportunity to inquire about their strengths and resources that have made this possible. If, on the other hand, they describe having the worst fights of their lives, the couple therapist can normalize the fights as a developmental event and offer suggestions for making the fights less toxic and damaging.

What Is the Life-cycle Perspective?

The notion that there are universal, predictable stages in human development has long been a cornerstone of the field of child development, as evidenced in the widely accepted writings of Erikson (1951) and Piaget and Inhelder (1969). It is a somewhat newer idea that adults continue to develop past college years (Dawber, 1980; Friedman & Martin, 2011; Levinson, 1978; Sheehy, 1976; Vaillant, 2012) and newer still that relationships in a family follow a developmental arc (McGoldrick, Preto, & Carter, 2016; Carter & McGoldrick, 1989).

One longitudinal study of 80 years duration (and still ongoing) has focused on both the individual lives of men, and later, on their marital relationships. The study is composed of two groups of men. The first is the Grant study, which began in 1938 as an attempt to study optimum health and potential by focusing on privileged and healthy men at Harvard: They were sophomores at the start, and now many are in their 90s. The second group, the Glueck cohort, made up of young men from low-income urban neighborhoods in Boston, was added in 1940.

Writing about this research, Vaillant (2012) cautions that "stage is a metaphor." While one can see clearly delineated stages in how the embryo develops, adult development is not nearly so step-wise and predictable. In particular, the life trajectories of both the privileged and the low-income men revealed that childhood experiences did not reliably predict what happens in the future. Lives did not unfold smoothly from strong, positive early experiences through happy mid-life and onward to a satisfying old age.

Those looking at resilience over the cycle also note the absence of lives progressing in lock-step from a negative start to a disastrous end nor from a charmed childhood to a ripe and happy old age. Rather, people have many opportunities to turn their lives around when a good marriage, or gratifying work, or the advent of parenthood can disrupt what seemed like a negative march through time (Walsh, 2016). Drawing on longitudinal studies, Werner and Smith (2011) also found that difficult early experience did not doom later-life trajectories. Rather, a supportive marriage or satisfying work could interrupt a negative start to life and catalyze a more positive spiral. This view suggests that stages do not need to be completed successfully before moving on to the next, but rather that each stage offers another chance at altering a couple's narrative.

Relationships have a beginning, middle, and end. Time is the river that flows through all couples' relationships. But rivers, like relationships, get dammed, form oxbows, make detours, circumvent obstacles, shoot over waterfalls, settle as swamps, and pick up and deposit detritus and sediment as they meander, so their journey is never a straight shot. Just as a river rushes, or meanders toward the ocean, so time propels every couple through terrain with recognizable landmarks. Time, or biological aging, has an impact on all aspects of a couple's life—work, sex, health, conflict, connection, and caregiving. There are six major life-cycle stages that couples typically traverse from dating to death, divorce, or separation. These stages are rooted in a westernized view of relationships and may look different across cultures and across historical periods (McGoldrick, Carter, & Preto, 2016; Carter & McGoldrick, 1989).[1]

- The first one begins with opening up to a stranger, falling in love, often cohabitating, and deciding to commit to a future together. The central task of this stage of courtship and commitment is for each member of the couple to separate enough from families of origin so that the couple can make decisions jointly.
- The second stage is the couple's transformation from a dyad to a triad, with the addition of a baby where work and relationship needs are renegotiated, and the couple makes room for a new person.
- Stage three is about maintaining the couple's bond at midlife as work commitments deepen, increased flexibility is required in parenting adolescent children, and aging parents may need caregiving.
- The fourth stage, now the longest adult stage, begins with children's leaving home and ends with the start of the couple's retirement.
- In the fifth stage, retirement, grandparenthood, and aging are the focus; couples' tasks include maintaining their connection in the face of health problems, adjusting to more time together, and finding meaning as time runs out.

---

[1] I am grateful for the seminal and ground-breaking work on life-cycle stages put forth by Monica McGoldrick, Nydia Garcia Preto, and Betty Carter over the last three decades.

- The sixth stage centers on the loss of the relationship through death, divorce, or separation.

This trajectory is, of course, not the only one that couples take, and not all couples traverse all these stages. Other transitions—like migration, traumatic losses, and disability—may be much more formative than these developmental ones. There are also many variations of life experience for couples who stay together on a long developmental arc. Three variations are particularly important in clinical practice. First, the inclusion of parenting in stages two, three, and four of the life-cycle stages requires that clinical attention also be provided to represent the experience of the many couples who will choose not to have children, but who stay married over the same period of time as couples with children. Second, the legalization of same-sex marriage (Supreme Court, 2015) is so recent that there is scant longitudinal data on long-term same-sex marriages, so we must wait for research data on how the developmental stages may differ or overlap with those of heterosexual couples. In the meantime, clinical knowledge and an emerging body of research on same-sex marriages can offer guidance about same-sex couples. Divorce and remarriage is a third normative variation over the life span. In the last 30 years, divorce has supplanted death as the endpoint for the majority of marriages. This shift has prompted some couple therapists to regard divorce as a normative life-cycle event that may be positive or negative (Pinsof, 2002).

Life-cycle theory posits that couples experience the most stress at the transition points, as one stage turns into another, and often as family members are added, as in marriage and the transition to parenthood, and lost, as during the launching stage and at the death of a spouse. When moving from one stage to the other, the organization of the couple must change. It is not, however, merely the transitioning from one stage to the other that creates strain on a relationship. If, in addition, there is an accumulation of stressors that coincides with a transition point, as when a couple is expecting a first child at the same time that the husband's mother is diagnosed with metastatic cancer, and the couple has to relocate to a new city without any supports, they may struggle. A transition point can also be exacerbated if it resonates with difficulty encountered in a previous generation at a similar stage of life, as when an expectant couple grew up in families where there were miscarriages or deaths of children. This couple may anticipate the transition to parenthood with an extra burden of anxiety and apprehension.

At the core of this life-cycle perspective is the notion that family relationships shape our identities, with each generation connected to the ones behind and ahead. The generations are mutually influencing and informing of one another so that is not only that parents guide their children's development, but it is also the case that children's unfolding lives reverberate in the life choices made by their parents and grandparents. Take, for example, the way that adolescents' burgeoning sexuality and dreams about their open-ended futures may inspire their middle-aged parents to take stock of their more limited time that lies ahead.

There are two other dimensions of time that are critical to an understanding of life-cycle theory. First is the historical context of each cohort of couples who is experiencing a particular life-cycle transition, as people born at a given time will share certain opportunities and sociopolitical experiences (Elder & Giele, 2009). Consider, for example, the cohort differences of same-sex couples born in 1990 who came of age seeing gay marriage legalized, compared with couples born in 1950 when gay and lesbian identities were often regarded as signs of mental illness, and sodomy laws could be used to criminalize individuals. When lesbian and gay teens were recently surveyed about their attitudes toward marriage and parenting, 92 percent of lesbian youth and 82 percent of gay youth stated that wanted to be in a long-term monogamous relationship within the next 10 years (D'Augelli, Redina, Grossman, & Sinclair, 2007), while more than half of these same young men and women stated that it was *very* or *extremely likely* that they would be raising children. These attitudes among current lesbian and gay youth stand in stark contrast to the closeted and constricted attitudes of similar youth in the 1950s whose best hopes for marriage and a family were to hide their identities and enter a heterosexual marriage.

The second dimension of time is the subjective one that all humans experience, an internal clock that tells whether one is traversing a given life stage at the expected time and provides an awareness of how much time one has left. Bernice Neugarten, a psychologist, is credited with identifying the notion that we each have a sense of what is a normal time to accomplish different stages of the life-cycle (Neugarten, 1979).

Comparing ourselves to friends, siblings, work colleagues, and parents, we have an idea of when is the best time to move in with a partner, marry, have a child, settle on a career, or retire. This sense of timeliness is historically constructed, contextualized by the experience of our families and by our particular cohort. So, for example, a pregnant medical student in her late 20s may feel *on time* in terms of her family's expectations, and in step with 21st century culture in general, but *early* compared with her cohort of medical students, who are largely postponing childbearing until completing their medical education. For another couple, having a child in their early 30s will feel *late* compared with their parents' histories of starting families in their early 20s. Neugarten made the observation that life-cycle transitions are made more difficult when they happen *off cycle*. For example, it is not children's leave-taking at midlife that creates a developmental crisis, but rather children's not leaving home when they are expected to do so, consistent with cultural norms or familial expectations.

According to the socioemotional selectivity theory, one's chronological age shapes an individual's choices of present and future goals (Carstensen, Isaacowitz, & Charles, 1999; Charles & Carstensen, 2009). People who are young and healthy tend to view the future as open-ended, prioritizing goals of gaining knowledge that can be deployed for future pursuits, while older people are more present-focused. Younger people are also more like likely to have a larger network of friends, than older people, who tend to focus on a smaller cohort of friends and families (Fung, Carstensen, & Lang, 2001). When time horizons are shorter, due either to old age or ill health, people tend to emphasize emotion and meaning and to pay selective attention toward positive rather than negative stimuli. When couples occupy two different perceptions of time, either because of a wide age difference or because one partner is facing a life-threatening illness, time itself can be an area of conflict.

Clinical Example: Not Age but Stage of Development

When Daphne and Martin[2] first came for couple therapy, I was initially struck by their sartorial dissimilarities—Martin was not afraid of color, from

---

[2] This case, as all others throughout the book, has been deidentified in order to protect the identity of my clients.

his boldly patterned socks to his bright orange shirt and green vest, while Daphne was dressed head to toe in black. Next, I noticed another contrast, and one that they warned me not to be judgmental about—a 40-year age difference. At 33, Daphne, a Euro-American woman, had just finished her graduate degree in art history and was looking for a job, while Martin, a 72-year-old Jewish artist and writer, was still working full-time with no plans to retire. There were more developmental asymmetries: Martin was at the height of his career and Daphne was just starting out; Martin had four children and several grandchildren, while Daphne was uncertain about whether she wanted to have any children; Martin had accumulated wealth, two houses, and an art collection, while Daphne was still living in graduate school housing; Martin was keenly aware of limited time and wanted to focus just on those projects and people whom he knew were interesting and compelling, while Daphne wanted to explore many new friendships and travel. Focusing on their developmental tasks, biological clocks, and relative sense of future time as points of difference gave a way to talk about their relationship. This focus also led us to look squarely at the power differences that their different developmental locations reveal. Age, parent status, money, and professional standing are power issues as well as developmental ones.

Daphne described her challenges in the relationship this way: "I feel like I'm fitting in to his life, his house, his family. If I weren't here, he'd be making the same decisions about his life. I'm not having an impact. He can't hear me unless I get angry and upset. I have spooned myself around his life. Being with him means that his relationship with his children will always be stronger than with me. The balance is off." Martin talked about the guilt he felt, inviting Daphne to share a life that would likely leave her widowed and childless when she was in her middle-age years. He was unwavering about his wish not to have a second family in his 70s.

And still, there were commonalities between them and ways their emotional needs were interlocking. They both had childhoods where they were left on their own, by parents with mental illness. Daphne had developed a strategy of not relying on anyone, but found that Martin was steady and trustworthy, the first man she could turn to for help and reassurance. This was the first time she did not worry about finances; consequently, she experienced a freedom to experiment with career options, and artistic pursuits, that she had yearned for as an adolescent and young adult. Martin, for his part, had always been the caretaker in his previous relationships, but with Daphne, Martin felt he could be vulnerable and expose his feelings in a way he could not when he was the sole provider of four children and adhering to more old-fashioned 1950s style versions of masculinity.

Daphne and Martin worked hard in couple therapy for over two years. Both felt that this was the most intimate relationship of their lives—they deeply loved and felt cherished by the other. Martin wanted to marry Daphne and told her so, but their developmental issues proved insurmountable. Some of these issues pertained to their different perspectives on time. Like many older individuals, Martin often wished to let go of their conflicts and focus instead on the positive aspects of their relationship, while Daphne was more interested in engaging in and working through conflict. Also congruent with those in late life, Martin wished to spend time with Daphne and a small group of friends and family he knew and loved already, while Daphne, with a more expansive future, was far more interested in making new friends, having adventures, and novel experiences. Most profoundly, their developmental differences pivoted around Daphne's wish to live on her own, so that she could develop her career out from under Martin's powerful shadow and decide whether she wanted a child. With much sadness, some regret, and deep affection, they parted ways.

Changing Social Forces Have Affected Life-cycle Stages

The length, definition, and even existence of different stages of the life cycle are shaped and influenced by larger social and historical forces. For example, over the last 100 years, the extending of life expectancy and the shrinking of family size have created the longest stage of adult development. Americans are living 30 years longer than they did 100 years ago. In 1900, life expectancy was 47 years, while today, about 75 percent of the population lives beyond their 65th birthday (Skolnick, 2013). The *launching* or *empty nest* stage is now the longest stage in adulthood, whereas it used to be the shortest one. When a woman had a large family, having a last child when she was in her 40s, she or her husband would likely die before they reached the empty nest stage. With couples now having fewer children, completing child-bearing earlier, and living longer, this stage, which begins when children leave home and ends with retirement, can be 20 or more years (see Chapter 5).

Definitions of marriage have experienced major revisions and edits over the last few decades. Most significant for Americans has been the legalization of same-sex marriage recognized in June 2015 by the U.S. Supreme Court. Leading up to this vote was Massachusetts' legalization of same-sex marriages in 2004, with 36 more states and the District of Columbia following suit by March 2015. As of 2015, 40 percent of all same-sex couples are married, while cohabiting and divorce rates are similar to those of different-sex couples (Gates, 2015). As many as 2 to 3.7 million children have an LGBT parent, but only about 200,000 are being raised by same-sex couples. In Chapters 2 through 7, clinical guidance will be offered for therapists working with same-sex couples navigating the different stages of the life cycle. These suggestions have been gathered from the author's clinical experience, interviews with couple therapists who work primarily with LGBT couples, and from the growing research in this area. Special attention will be paid to the observations of researchers and clinicians in Massachusetts working with same-sex couples who have had the opportunity to have the longest legal marriages.

Legalization of same-sex marriage is not the only major shift in the marital landscape. The age at which men and women marry for the first time has increased significantly over the past 30 years. From 1980 to 2016, the median age of first marriage for men rose from 24.7 to 29.5, and for women, from 22.0 to 27.4 years of age (U.S. Census, 2016). Not only are young men and women postponing marriage, but also more young adults are choosing cohabitation over marriage. Marriage rates are at an all-time low. Between 1980 and 2016, the proportion of married men has declined from 63 to 53 percent, and for married women, from 59 to 51 percent (U.S. Census Bureau, 2017). And, it is not just marriage that is being postponed. Many women are delaying childbearing due to educational opportunities or difficulties finding a partner, with higher rates of infertility as an unintended consequence.

While many couples struggle with unwanted childlessness due to infertility, there are growing numbers of couples who choose to remain childfree. In 2006, 20 percent of women ages 40 to 44 had never had a child, compared to half that number in 1976 (Dye, 2008; Osborne, 2003), numbers that include women who are childless both voluntarily and involuntarily. Married couples who choose not to have children do so for a variety of reasons: they may want to remain more mobile, with ample time and flexibility to invest in their careers; they may want to maintain a more intimate marriage; they may feel unsuited to parenthood or feel worried that they will pass along a difficult genetic loading; others may postpone childrearing decisions to a time when biological reproduction is no longer an option. Regardless of whether by choice or by default, childless couples tend to be better educated, more likely to be urban-dwellers, and less likely to be religiously affiliated (DeOllos & Kapinus, 2002; Keizer, Dykstra, & Jansen, 2008). Over many studies, researchers have found that couples without children experience similar or higher levels of wellbeing at most stages of the life cycle than couples who are parents (Koropeckyji-Cox, Pienta, & Brown, 2007; Nomaguchi & Milkie, 2003; Pudrovska, 2008; Umberson, Pudrovska, & Reczek, 2010; Wenger, Dykstra, Melkas, & Knipscheer, 2007; Zhang & Hayward, 2001). In general, couples who did not choose to be childless were less happy and more depressed than those who were voluntarily childfree. In addition, gender and marital status have an impact on wellbeing. For example, childlessness had the biggest negative impact on those who were widowed, particularly among men (Zhang & Hayward, 2001).

Postponement of marriage and childbearing, increased numbers of couples not having children, more couples cohabiting with and without children, and legalization of same-sex marriage are only some of the changes to current living arrangements. We are also seeing more gender equity in modern marriages. Most married women work outside the home, contributing to a rise of shared decision-making as a cultural value. There has been a dramatic increase in dual-earner couples, such that 70 percent of couples with children under the age of 18 are dual earners, up from one-quarter in 1960 (Pew Research Center, 2015). It is not just women who are contributing to the gender rebalancing of home and work roles. The number of stay-at-home fathers has doubled over the last 30 years (Livingston, 2014), while men in general are playing a more active role in childrearing. In the last two decades, fathers have more than doubled the time spent on household chores and tripled the time spent with children (Parker, 2016). Several studies suggest that couples in egalitarian marriages experience higher marital quality (Amato, Booth, Johnson, & Rogers, 2007; Frisco & Williams, 2003; Kamp Dush & Taylor, 2012).

There are, however, gaping class divides that undermine this picture of increased equity. Highly educated women are more likely to marry than less educated women. Of those with a college education, 88 percent of women aged 33 to 44 are married, and their divorce rate is 17 percent in the first 10 years. By contrast, 79 percent of women in the same age bracket with less than a high school diploma have married, and the divorce rate for them in the first decade of marriage is 50 percent (McGoldrick, Carter, & Preto, 2016; Stevenson & Wolfers, 2007). Low-income couples are more likely to move in with each other quickly, have children at an earlier age, and move on if the relationship does not work out. Children living in cohabitating or single-parent families are two to three times more likely to be living in poverty than children living in married families. It is ironic, indeed, that as marriage becomes more equitable for some, the class divide around marriage and divorce rates grows more pronounced.

The intersection of race and marriage reveals that there are significant differences in marriage rates among White, African–American, Hispanic, and Asian couples. For couples who married for the first time between 2006 and 2010, the chance of a 20-year marriage is nearly 70 percent for Asian women, but only 36 percent for Black women and 50 percent for both White and Hispanic women (Wang, 2015).

Over recent decades, marriage rates have dropped much more precipitously for African–Americans than for Whites. In 1960, 78 percent of African–American households included a married couple, while 40 years later, the rate had plummeted to only 16 percent (Pinderhughes, 2002). By stark comparison, the marriage rate decreased much less dramatically from 74 to 56 percent among White couples during that same period. When children are included in the family calculus, the racial divide is also obvious. About three-fifths of African–American children will grow up in a single-parent family as compared with only one-quarter of White children (US Census Bureau, 2017).

These racial disparities are not reflected in attitudes toward marriage. Blacks and Whites value marriage similarly, and Blacks are significantly more likely than Whites to disapprove of divorce. Despite these beliefs, rates of singlehood are high among African–Americans, in part due to a male shortage that is attributable to higher rates of poverty, incarceration, and drug use (Chambers & Kravitz, 2011; McKinnon, 2003; Teachman, Tedrow & Croder, 2000). Added to these factors is higher unemployment among African–American men, a deterrent to marriage.

Family composition has also changed over the past 30 years. Fewer than half of the children under the age of 18 years live with two married parents, and about 40 percent live with single or cohabitating parents (Livingston, 2014). Increasingly, marriage and parenting are becoming uncoupled. Adding to the complexity of family life is the number of Americans living in multigenerational households, which doubled between 1980 and 2012 (Fry & Passel, 2014). As a consequence of later marriage rates and longer educational paths among higher-income young adults, as well as declining employment and wages among many lower-income young adults, 25 percent of adults ages 25 to 34 lived with their parents in 2015 as compared to only 11 percent in 1980.

Divorce Is as Common an End to Marriage as Death

In 1900, two-thirds of marriages ended within 40 years as a result of one partner's death. The year 1974 was a watershed as it marked the point at which marriages were more likely to end in divorce than in death (Hagestad, 1988). Spikes in divorce occur at predictable points during the life-cycle, with the largest one after five to seven years of marriage, and another at 15 to 17 years of marriage (Gottman & Levensen, 2000). Recent surveys suggest that, while divorce rates among younger couples are declining, the divorce rate among couples in their 50s and older doubled between 1990 and 2010 (Brown & Lin, 2012). This spike may be due to a cohort effect of Baby Boomers who were responsible for the increased divorce rate in the 70s continuing their patterns of high marital instability in subsequent marriages (Kennedy & Ruggles, 2014). Or, the rise in divorce in older individuals may represent changing social and historical forces, such as a longer life expectancy that makes a many-decade marriage too heavy a burden, or increased gender equity that allows more women the freedom to leave a marriage with her own income and retirement benefits. In any case, if half of divorces occur within the first seven years of marriage, another quarter of all divorces occur in couples who are 50 or older. Divorce rates are inextricably linked to class, as well as to age. For college-educated women, there is almost an 80 percent chance of still being married after two decades, while for women with a high school education or less, their chances are only 40 percent (Wang, 2015).

Clinical Example: The Use of a Developmental Reframe

The developmental lens not only provides context and orients the couple therapist to common challenges but can itself be an intervention. By introducing a previous stage of life that was skipped over, a developmental reframe can shift a couple from blaming one another toward adopting a dyadic and nonjudgmental view of their current difficulties.

When Maria and Ralph, an African–American couple in their early 30s, came to a Boston-area clinic, they complained of feeling like siblings, the kind who squabble and then go their own way. Married for five years, they had two daughters, Anna age 5 and Sophia age 2. Although the reason they gave for their clinic visit was their older daughter's second expulsion from a pre-school due to biting other children, other difficulties—more typical of couples who are older and have been married for decades—came tumbling out. They met seven years earlier, shortly after the death of Maria's mother. Not long after that, Maria was diagnosed with early-stage breast cancer for which she was treated with radiation, chemotherapy, and surgery. During cancer treatment, the couple moved in with one another and only a month later, Ralph's mother, following a fall that was the first symptom of Alzheimer's, moved in and continued to live with them until her death a year ago.

The couple sought a diagnosis for their daughter, and they wanted help managing her temper outbursts at home. As their therapist, I was torn between focusing on their current problem and wondering how their shaky start as a couple might be interfering with their difficulties collaborating as parents. As part of my feedback after the first few sessions, I offered a developmental reframe. "It is no wonder that you are feeling more like siblings than like partners as you face a parenting challenge with Anna. It sounds like life threw crisis after crisis at you, like the death of a parent, a serious medical illness, and the care-taking of an ill parent that most couples don't have to deal with right out of the gate. Because you had to deal with challenges more typical of older couples who already know each other well, you skipped an important developmental stage—creating an identity as a couple.

"In addition to figuring out a good plan for helping Anna, I'd like to suggest that we do some time travel in here. Let's go back to the developmental stage you missed out on and take some time to have conversations you might have had if you hadn't had to race ahead. For example, 'Where do you want to live?' 'How do you resolve disagreements?' 'Who are your friends?' 'What role, if any, does religion or spirituality play in your lives?' 'What rituals, like dinner or holiday get-togethers, are important to you?' 'What do you like to do together when you have leisure time?' 'What is important to you as you envision a future together?' These are just a few topics that we might discuss."

The developmental reframe is a normalizing intervention that recasts a current problem as indicating that a couple bypassed an important earlier stage or has gotten stuck at a prior stage. With Maria and Ralph, their current distant and contentious relationship was interfering with their ability to collaborate on a parenting plan for their elder daughter. By offering an empathic explanation for their difficulties—that they got derailed in developing their relationship by having to take on responsibilities more typical of an older couple—they were offered a way forward that sidestepped any assignments of blame. This developmental reframe also gave an entry point to talk about the losses they experienced together, and how their caretaking of each other had shaped their current relationship.

In the coming chapters, the developmental perspective will next be applied to each stage of a couple's lifespan. Starting with courtship and the decision to marry or commit to one another, we will explore the research on the transition to marriage with an eye to better understanding this opening act. We will look at common presentations for therapy and make suggestions for questions and interventions that a couple therapist can offer to help couples as they initially embark on a life together.

CHAPTER 2

Transition to Being a Couple

Dating, Partner Selection, and Making a Long-Term Commitment

Marriage begins as a psychotherapy project. We all get married hoping that our partner will be to us all the things our parents weren't.
—Whitaker & Napier (1977)

Love is an act of the imagination. For some of us, it will be the greatest creative triumph of our lives.
—Person (1989)

Becoming a couple is one of the most complicated transitions in the life cycle. The process that begins with dating and courtship, then progresses to the decision to cohabitate, marry or to make a long-term commitment, often moves on to the navigation of wedding plans, and finally traverses to the first years of serious commitment or marriage presents multiple challenges and brings many couples to therapy. This stage accounts for more than a third of all couple therapy referrals at a major teaching hospital and is second only to the transition to parenthood as a time in the life cycle for relational distress.[1] An added weight to this stage is the rosy cast that cultures imbue it with: Countless movies and novels suggest that a wedding marks the beginning of a happily-ever-after narrative. This misrepresentation of the stage as exclusively positive and romantic is an extra burden on burgeoning relationships.

Many tasks get packed into this stage. As couples move toward long-term commitment, they must figure out how to negotiate together the

---

[1] Fishel records of couples referrals made to Massachusetts General Hospital, 2015–2017, unpublished.

many decisions that each one used to make as a single person or within their families of origin. Some of these decisions include figuring out the particulars around eating, sleeping, fighting, celebrating holidays, and having sex, as well as how to use space, time, and money (McGoldrick et al., 2016). On top of that, couples, particularly those in Western cultures, must reconfigure their relationships with parents, siblings, and friends to make room for the primacy of their partner, placing that relationship ahead of all others. Often, other family members push back against the introduction of a new member, sometimes the first since the birth of children decades earlier. A redrawing of the boundaries and loyalties between generations commonly defines this stage.

In this chapter, we will focus primarily on the transition to marriage as the marker for becoming a couple, even though many couples will choose to move in with one another, buy real estate, or have a baby as a cap-stone of their commitment to one another. In the United States, while marriage rates have fallen in recent decades and cohabitation rates have risen, the share of cohabitating adults is still not that high, comprising only 7 percent of U.S. adults in 2016 (Pew Research Center, 2016). The focus on marriage, rather than on other possible indicators of commitment is also based on the steady salience of marriage as a cultural goal, even among millennials (Hymowitz, Carroll, Wilcox, & Kaye, 2013), and on decades of research linking marriage to psychological, health, and financial bene-fits (Lee & Payne, 2010; Lin & Brown, 2012; Waite & Gallagher, 2000). Married couples, compared with their unmarried single, dating, or cohabi-tating counterparts, live longer, report higher levels of happiness, and enjoy more social and community resources (Brown, Bulanda, & Lee, 2012; Lee & Paine, 2010; Wienke & Hill, 2009). Even when controlling for rela-tionship satisfaction, married couples have the highest levels of wellbeing, followed by cohabitating couples and those in steady dating relationships (Lee & Bulanda, 2005; Wienke & Hill, 2008). The benefits of marriage, over other relationships, derive from the higher level of commitment and the stronger outlook toward the future (Kamp Dush, & Amato, 2005).

Since same-sex marriage has been legalized, there is a growing body of literature indicating that marriage confers the same benefits to mar-ried lesbian couples (Ducharme & Kollar, 2012) and married gay and bisexual couples (Riggle, Rostosky, & Horne, 2010; Wight, LeBlanc, & Badgett, 2013). Furthermore, in studies conducted since the legalization of same-sex marriage, married lesbian, gay, and bisexual individuals have been found to be significantly less distressed than those not in a legal same-sex relationship (Wight, LeBlanc, & Badgett, 2013).

While marriage confers many benefits, it does not do so equitably. As discussed in the previous chapter, notable differences in rates of marriage and divorce exist along class and race lines. The growing class and race divides in marriage rates raise the question of whether some of the health and psychological benefits attributed to marriage may be due, at least in part, to being wealthier and to having access to other forms of privilege.

Common Presentations

The sexual orientation, culture, class, and race background of a couple will differentially shape their attitudes toward marriage. For example, some same-sex couples eschew marriage as a patriarchal institution and prefer to create their own relational guidelines, while other same-sex couples come out to their families at the same time that they announce their wedding plans. A growing number of straight and gay couples will choose to live together, rather than marry, in order to preserve autonomy, or to avoid the expense and burden of a wedding. Still, other couples, for example from traditional Asian families, will arrive at marriage through an arrangement, decided on by their parents. The Western emphasis on separation from family of origin as a hallmark of marriage will be much less important for these couples. Despite these many variations, there are some commonalities in how couples present for therapy on the cusp of serious long-term commitment or marriage. Many of these presentations revolve around the challenges of bridging the customs, rituals, and family backgrounds of two individuals who are hoping to make a life together.

The most common clinical presentations are attributable to *tensions between the couple and one or both families of origin*, which may bubble up around the wedding planning.

Samantha and Roger, for example, came from very different families: She had grown up with wealth and privilege in a Protestant family whose ancestors had come to the United States many generations ago. She attended private schools and an elite college. By contrast, Roger grew up in a working-class Polish family with immigrant parents, attended public school, and was the first of his family to attend college, a state university where he commuted from home.

When Roger told his parents that he planned to marry Samantha, they were happy for him but privately worried that Samantha's family would dominate the wedding planning and then go on to capture Roger and future grandchildren, leaving them out in the cold. In an effort not to be sidelined, Roger's parents made frequent demands about the wedding: to invite guests whom Roger had never met, to dictate the type of ceremony the couple should have, and to bad-mouth the future in-laws. Roger, who had always smiled and acquiesced to his parents and then quietly done his own thing, could not maintain this strategy with his fiancée, who insisted that he stand up to his family and set limits on their wishes. The wedding planning offered a chance for the couple to set clear boundaries around their relationship and to figure out how they wanted to stay connected to both sides of the family as they moved forward. Samantha was able to help Roger be more direct with his family about not liking their bossiness, while Roger was able to talk to Samantha about not wanting to adopt all the values and privileges of her family.

Another common presentation at this stage is the *partner who discloses difficult information after the engagement or early in the marriage* with the attitude of "*Now that you have committed to me, you have a right to know,*" about something that felt too shameful to disclose earlier, like a mental illness diagnosis, an abortion, or sexual abuse.

Through tears, Aisha began couple therapy by recounting her distress when Naveed, her fiancé, had recently told her that another woman had kissed him during the first week that they had started dating. She announced that because of this kiss, four years ago, she was calling off their engagement.

The kiss, however, was not really the challenging disclosure. When asked what this kiss meant to her, Aisha revealed that she had been raped as a young girl in Pakistan. She worried that she would never be able to enjoy having intercourse, and therefore, she saw kissing as the most intimate act that she could ever expect to enjoy. With this new disclosure, Naveed now understood why she was so upset about a kiss that had seemed so long ago and so unimportant to him. They were able to focus on understanding the real disclosure of Aisha's early sexual abuse.

Couples may also present at this stage of the life-cycle with *concerns about their own or their partner's capacity for fidelity and commitment.*

One couple came to see me six months into their marriage. Astaire, a surgeon, had told Beth on their wedding eve that he had had several sexual relationships with patients and nurses during the past year. If she wanted to call off the wedding, he said, he would totally understand. In addition to feeling devastated by this revelation, Beth did not also want to feel humiliated by publicly announcing that the wedding was canceled to their 100 assembled guests. Instead, she staggered through the ceremony and was pretty sure that they were coming to couple therapy to begin a divorce process. Indeed, ending the relationship was our focus.

The *disillusioning shift* that nascent couples make—from believing they are kindred souls to discovering instead that they have clashing perspectives, feelings, and beliefs—can bring a couple to therapy. This shift may be accompanied by profound disappointment and a fair amount of fear.

"You aren't who I thought you were. I thought you really understood me, without even having to explain myself," Steve, a 42-year-old nurse said in the first few minutes about his husband Michael, a 40-year-old teacher. They had been married for less than a year when they came to couple therapy with a sense that their connection had shifted in unforeseen ways. As Steve put it, "We have no process for fighting, and this is particularly hard when we have so many differences to discuss."

Another presentation is a *pile-up of stressful events* around the transition to marriage that then overwhelm the couple or detract from the process of couple formation.

Married for less than a year, Jason and Maddy were struggling with a cascade of life events: Jason, returning from a six-month deployment to Iraq, learned that Maddy had been diagnosed with an autoimmune disease that made intercourse painful. Jason's father had lost his job and was clinically depressed, and his parents were leaning on him for help, at the very time when he needed to be loosening his bonds to his family of origin in order to create his own new marriage. Therapy included a meeting between Jason, his parents, and siblings to set boundaries and shift the weight of responsibility off of Jason.

Clinical Questions and Interventions

Clinicians can find guideposts to working with new couples by understanding the growing body of research that identifies risk factors for divorce that can appear as early as the transition to marriage. The findings can be divided into three categories: issues of timing, family-of-origin matters, and relational dilemmas. The summary that follows is not meant as a checklist where the more risk factors the couple has, the more likely they are to divorce. Rather, each risk factor can orient the clinician to explore an area with the couple, and in many instances, can point to preventive strategies to strengthen the relationship.

Issues of Timing

The Couple Marries at a Young Age

Studies suggest that couples who marry before age 20 in the United States face special challenges, even when controlling for variables like parental marital instability and educational attainment (Booth & Edwards, 1985). Entering marriage during teenage years may be motivated by a wish to run away from a difficult family situation or to look for a family that one never had. In either case, a teenage couple will not have had the time to achieve much independence prior to entering into marriage. On a practical level, a young couple's separation from parents may also be undermined by having to be financially dependent on them. Finally, lack of fidelity is the greatest source of dissatisfaction for very young couples. It may be difficult to maintain fidelity at the very time of the life cycle when the drive for sexual experimentation peaks.

Pregnancy Before or Within the First Year of Marriage

The challenge of a pregnancy early in marriage is that it can interfere with the working through of all the other tasks involved in the transition to marriage (Christensen, 1963; Bacon, 1974). If a couple has to figure out how to take care of a baby while also creating a foundation for themselves as a couple, it can overwhelm their time and resources. This would be like a child learning to nurse and walk at the same time. When a woman is in her late 30s or 40s, however, she may not have the luxury to wait a few years before trying to get pregnant, even if this means consolidating two life stages into one short time period. Therapists can help couples make time in therapy and at home to have conversations about the multiple decisions of early coupledom, conversations that can be distinguished from those required of new parents (as discussed in Chapter 3).

Of course, a pregnancy is not the only event that can intrude on a couple's early bonding. Other events, like a serious medical illness, can also overwhelm and derail a budding relationship. For older couples, the notion that one member's illness is affecting both members and needs to be faced together can be a stretch when the couple is just starting to build a sense of their shared identity.

Sex Starts Right Away

Data from the National Longitudinal Study of Adolescent Health reveals that about half of premarital young adult couples become sexually involved within the first month of dating, while another 25 percent initiate sex one to three months into a dating relationship (Sassler & Kamp Dush, 2009). Some studies suggest that the rapid entry into a sexual relationship may interrupt the period of courtship, as well as exploration of each other and decision-making about their compatibility (Sassler, Addo, & Lichter, 2012). Even casual sex can feel like love because the stimulation of genitals releases an upsurge in dopamine, triggering the brain circuits of romantic love (Fisher, 2004).

Gender differences have been reported in a study of 600 low- to moderate- income couples: for men, the speed of initiating sexual activity was unrelated to the later quality of the relationship, while women who had sex early in a relationship were later less satisfied with the marital quality (Busby, Carroll, & Willoughby, 2010; Sassler et al., 2012). Premarital sex itself, however, is not a predictor of elevated divorce rates (Teachman, 2003).

The rapid entry into sexual relationships may be part of another pattern.

Sliding Versus Deciding

Not only do most couples have sex before marriage, but most also live together prior to marriage. Some researchers have focused on how couples move from each step toward deepening commitment—from having sex, to moving in together, to getting engaged, to having a wedding, to having children (Stanley, Rhoades, & Markman, 2006). Some couples *slide* into the decision, letting happenstance or inertia be their guides. Take, for example, the couple who decides to move in together because one person's lease is up and "it will be easier not to pay two rents when we're spending several nights with each other anyway." By contrast, *deciders* are couples who talk about an upcoming transition and make an intentional choice together. Instead of forgetting to use birth control and accidentally becoming pregnant, a decider couple would plan to start trying to conceive once both members of the couple have finished school and found work.

The findings from this body of research suggest that couples who slide through their relationship transitions have poorer marital quality than those who make intentional decisions about major milestones. Financially strapped couples may be more prone to slide into their joint decisions because of economic factors like housing crises or a job transition. The problem with sliding is that each transition limits options, which is well and good if the couple chose those constraints. But, if the constraints come along after cohabitation or after having a child, and were not chosen, the couple may feel trapped.

Sliding can also feel like an easier path, if only because deciding on a mate choice is so weighty: Along with education and occupation, partner selection is among the first major adult decisions two young people make, and anything that is considered on a time horizon of *forever* can be daunting. Reviewing the history of how the couple made decisions as individuals and how extended family members have made decisions can offer a helpful context. Additionally, a therapist can use the following exercise with a couple who is ambivalent about whether to marry: During one session (and followed-up during the week), the couple can talk together about all the ways that their life would be different if they were married; then the next week (in therapy and during the week), the couple can talk together about all the ways their life would be different if they decided to separate. Rather than continue living in an ambiguous state, they can push their experience of commitment or dissolution, and they can explore it at the same time, together. Topics might include:

- "How will your relationships with family members change if you marry or separate?"
- "What fights will you still be having?"

- "How will each of your work lives be affected if you stay together or split up?"
- "What will need to change if you marry? And, what will you have to learn to live with?"
- "What will you each miss if you separate? How will you each think back on your relationship?"

The Couple Makes Decisions About Commitment to Each Other Soon After a Significant Loss

There are few psychological processes as mysterious as the choice of a love partner and the timing of that choice. Psychodynamic theorists posit that mate selection is unconsciously motivated by one's experiences in the family of origin: One may choose a partner to take over the aspects of emotional life that are challenging, as when someone from a very strict and rule-bound family falls for an emotionally expressive individual who cries and laughs with abandon; or one may try to recreate a painful family relationship in the hopes of making it turn out differently in marriage, as when someone with an abusive parent chooses an abusive partner; or one may attempt to re-enact a positive familial relationship by choosing a partner who resembles a beloved parent or sibling.

Ethel Spector Person, a psychoanalyst who wrote a seminal work on love, observed that falling in love is an act of the imagination, a process that starts inside individuals as they reciprocally project and try to fulfill their deepest longings and oldest dreams by finding someone who is a good-enough template for these desires (Person, 1989). As for the timing, Person argues that there are moments of ripeness and openness to love: in the face of separation (for example, at the start of a military tour of duty or at the end of college or medical school); when away from home (for example, a shipboard romance, or at a conference); or in the experience of loss (for example, after a parent falls ill or dies). It is this last option, when couples meet or marry around a loss of another important person that can be problematic for the start of a long-term relationship. Perhaps, when marital choices are made around the loss of a beloved family member, there will be increased needs to be met by one's partner, and more of a tendency to distort the partner, in an effort to reconstruct the lost relationship (Hepworth, Ryder, & Dreyer, 1984; Ryder, 1970).

Questions that reflect issues of *Timing*:

- "What was the first spark between the two of you? How did you know that you wanted to get to know the other? Was there anything going on in your lives or in the lives of your extended family that accelerated, complicated, or contributed to that process? Any significant losses around the time of your courtship and decision to marry?"
- "How did you make the decision to move in with each other, to get engaged or to get married? What did you learn about each other through that process?
  - How did your family respond to those decisions?
  - If you do not remember having those conversations, could we talk now about how you are making decisions regarding who your friends will be, how much time you will spend alone versus together, what religion if any you will observe, how often you want to visit with family?"
- With a couple who married very young, "What are some ways that you feel that you have separated from your parents, other than getting married?" "What are some things you are doing and thinking about to continue to develop and grow as a person?"

Family-of-Origin Issues

Out-of-Sync Sibling Relationships

A body of research predicts marital compatibility on the basis of the couple's sibling relationships (Toman, 1993). In a different-sex couple, if each partner grew up with siblings of the opposite gender, then research suggests that they come to marriage with a relational advantage. Additionally, if each member of the couple occupied different birth-order positions in their families growing up, they can then accommodate to one another in complementary, rather than competitive ways. So, for example, it may be salutary for an older sister of brothers to marry a younger brother of sisters. In this scenario, both husband and wife come to the marriage with a template for negotiating conflict and having fun with someone of the opposite sex, and as a bonus, they do not compete with one another as either the bossy elder or the pampered younger child.

Carrying Forward Childhood Experiences and Roles

While this research about siblings is interesting, there is a larger clinical message here. Each member comes to marriage with his or her own family history, including experiences and relationships that they want to carry forward, as well as those best left behind. The couple therapist can work with burgeoning relationships much like a lead test scientist who checks for toxic levels of the soil left by previous homeowners. Both members of the couple can be invited to explore their relationships to siblings and parents, the way nurture and anger were expressed, the ways that dinners and holidays were celebrated, and then decide as a couple what will be replicated. They can also identify what vulnerabilities were passed down from their childhood families. Like the lead-test scientist, the therapist helps the couple explore the soil they will be growing their new relationship in.

For same-sex couples, conversations about family of origin are more complicated, as most lesbian, gay, bisexual, and transgender (LGBT) children do not have parents who share their same status. Unlike children born Black or Jewish, almost no LGBT children grow up with parents who can help them develop a positive minority identity. For LGBT adults in intimate relationships, they will have to look elsewhere than their own families for examples of same-sex relationships (Addison & Coolhart, 2015). In addition to asking about family of origin, couple therapists will also want to ask about family of choice, or those individuals who are part of the couple's social network.

Parental Divorce

Several longitudinal studies indicate that the children who grew up with parents who divorced, themselves face an increased risk of divorcing later on. In one study, parental divorce doubled the chances for their offspring's marital instability, particularly if the parents had had low levels of discord before divorcing (Amato & DeBoer, 2001; Kobrin & Waite, 1984). Gender seems to contribute to a person being uncertain about the future of marriage at the engagement stage. Daughters, more than sons, of divorced parents enter marriage with more trepidation about being able to overcome marital difficulties (Whitton et al., 2008). This gender difference may be attributed to women being more attuned to their parents' divorce when it occurs and then carrying this awareness into their own marriages, so that they are more conscious of marriage's fragility. In addition to asking about parental divorce, clinicians would be wise to ask about parental violence, substance abuse, and infidelity, as these behaviors may continue to wield influence and worry in the next generation.

Couple Elopes or Has A Wedding Without Family or Friends

A wedding, whether a pot luck in an open field or a black-tie event at a fancy hotel, is a vitally important ritual. The planning of a wedding is a time-limited, choreographed opportunity to work out the merging of two families and to mark the advent of the couple becoming their own new family. In the planning, many decisions are made—who will pay? who will decide who gets invited? who will preside? will it be formal, religious, or casual?—and this process is both a reflection of family process and a chance to work through how two families with their own cultures, histories, and beliefs will come together. The wedding itself allows for the expression of deep, often contradictory feelings such as the joy of two people embarking on a new life together and the loss of the original family units. Perhaps most important, friends and families witness the couple's vows, and this witnessing helps to contain and reinforce the couple's ongoing commitment to each other. It can be helpful for the therapist to remind couples that the process of planning a wedding will serve them well in the future: If conflicts do not get worked out through the wedding planning, they may continue to percolate in an open-ended way into the future.

For same-sex couples, the wedding may bring to the fore the issue of making their relationship public to friends, family, and work colleagues. As with heterosexual couples, the decision to marry introduces some pressure to decide for couples in a long-term relationship: Is this good enough to be made legal or does it need to change, or end? In addition, many same-sex couples critique weddings and marriage in general as a heteronormative institution that they would like to be free from.

Different Family Backgrounds

While all marriages are cross-cultural, in that they bring together two people who were raised in different family cultures, marriages composed of two people who differ ethnically, racially, and religiously face additional complexity (Rastogi & Thomas, 2008). Since 1967, when the Supreme Court ruled that marriage across racial lines was legal throughout the country, there has been an uptick in intermarriage, with one in six Americans married to someone with a different race or ethnicity (Pew Research Center, 2017). These couples can be encouraged to value each other's differences and approach the other's cultural history and identity with interest. For some couples, these differences will be a source of curiosity, enabling each member to feel that his or her life experience is expanded and enriched by learning from the other. For other couples, these differences can be the source of misunderstanding or, worse, the person with less privilege may feel dominated or denigrated by the other.

Family-of-Origin Disapproval

In some families, there is parental disapproval of their child's choice of partner. Sometimes, this disapproval is rooted in the parents' distress that their child has chosen a partner at all, as this signals that their child is separating from them. Parental disapproval may also be tied to fears or prejudice when the mate choice belongs to another religious, ethnic, or racial group. A child's choice of someone different from the parents may be experienced as a rejection or betrayal of the family of origin, or may reveal outright prejudice. Exploring issues of separation in the current generation and the previous ones can help bring additional perspective and context. In addition, in most families, there have been examples over the generations of mate choices who were regarded as different, in terms of class, educational background, region of the country, or other dimensions. It can be normalizing for the couple to bring forth (and perhaps share with their parents) family stories about previous partner choices that expanded what was familiar.

Despite the widespread cultural shifts in acceptance of same-sex marriage, individuals still encounter homophobia in their families, work places, and communities. It is important to determine the differences between partners in *outness*—how long each has identified as gay or lesbian—and whether each has come out in different realms of their lives, such as family, work, and friends (Green & Mitchell, 2015; Otis, Rostosky, Riggle, & Hamrin, 2006). Anxiety about LGBT prejudice negatively relates to relationship satisfaction (Otis et al., 2006). Partners can be encouraged to "dispute, deconstruct, and subvert society's prejudicial views, rather than continue to internalize or be limited to them," in a manner that is similar to the narrative technique of *externalizing the problem* (Green & Mitchell, 2015, p. 494). In other words, homonegativity, both internalized and located in the family, is the destructive problem, rather than sexual orientation itself.

Questions about *family-of-origin* issues:

- "Tell me about the families you grew up in. What do you most want to carry forward from your families, and what, if anything, do you want to leave behind?"
- "Did you have or do you plan to have a wedding with family and with friends? If yes, how did or how are the preparations going? Any challenges around who gets invitations, who pays, who makes decisions, whether there will be a religious or civilian officiate? Have the two families met, and if so, how did that go?"
- "If there was a divorce in one or both families of origin, what is your understanding now of why your parents ended their marriage? How did you understand it at the time? Sometimes, children of divorce worry that they may not have the confidence or the ability to make a marriage last. Do you have any of those fears? What have you learned through observation or by talking to your parents about how to keep a marriage on track?"

- "Are there differences in background, in terms of class, religion, race, ethnicity, or age between the two of you? When were you first aware of them? How have these differences presented any challenges for the two of you? Have these differences been the source of interest and richness in your relationship?"
- "Which aspects of your racial or ethnic heritage are important to you? Have your families of origin had concerns about these differences? Do you or your family experience racism or stereotyping as a member of a racial group? Do you have relatives or ancestors who were persecuted or persecuted others? How has your family handled these painful memories?"
- For same-sex couples, "How do you think your sexual orientation affected your relationships with your parents and siblings when you were growing up? Describe your process of coming out to your family. Is there anyone in your family who does not know about your sexual orientation? Have you introduced your partner to your family? How have they responded?"

Relational Dilemmas

Infidelity in the First Two Years of Marriage

While infidelity is a risk factor for divorce at any stage of the life cycle, it is especially damaging when it occurs in the first two years of marriage (Pittman, 1990). Early infidelity can undermine the most basic sense of commitment and may belie a lack of attachment to the partner. In Pittman's research, he found that most of the marriages that had secret affairs in the first two years ended in divorce and the few that endured continued to be marked by later infidelities.

Couples who begin their marriage with a shared agreement about having extra-marital partners are a different story. A growing number of heterosexual couples are negotiating open marriages that allow for multiple partners. For many gay couples, negotiating the parameters of polyamory is more of a community preference (Green & Mitchell, 2015). According to Dr. Larry Rosenberg, a psychologist with 30 years of clinical practice, "there is a range of monogamous exclusivity in gay couples. They may start out monogamous then open it up, secretly, or by agreement—when one is travelling or by bringing in other sexual partners."[2] In same-sex as well as different-sex couples, it is secrecy about other partners that is most damaging.

Physical Aggression

Physical aggression is fairly prevalent during early marriage and highly predictive of divorce (Jacobson & Gottman, 2007; Rogge & Bradbury, 1999). Aggression may accompany other variables, like alcohol and drug abuse (Vaillant, 2012), psychopathology, and difficulty controlling anger, which are also corrosive to intimate relationships. Questions about substance abuse, impulse control, and anger management should always be asked as part of assessing safety in couples.

How Couples Fight

Over more than 30 years of researching newlywed couples, John Gottman and his colleagues have found that how couples fight early on forecasts their long-term marital stability (Carrere & Gottman, 1999; Gottman, Coan, Carrere, & Swanson, 1998). When couples are asked to re-enact a fight, there are several features of that fight that predict which couples are still together a decade later:

- A 5 to 1 ratio of positive-to-negative interactions during a conflict predicted couples who stayed together, compared with a 0.8 to 1 positive-to-negative ratio of unhappily married couples (Gottman & Levensen, 2002). Also important were the partners' decision to end a conflict with a return to positive comments about the relationship.
- The absence of *The four horsemen of the Apocalypse*, which are: criticism (placing blame in a way that points out a character defect); stonewalling (listener withdraws or does not respond); defensiveness (skirting responsibility for a problem); and

---

[2] Dr. Larry Rosenberg, personal communication, Cambridge MA, March 3, 2017.

contempt (talking in a way to sound superior or like your partner is bad or stupid, often accompanied by a non-verbal eye-roll or lip curl) (Gottman & Silver, 2016).

- The presence of repair comments during a conflict, such as "My reaction was too strong. Let me try again" or "I'm getting worried, scared." The path into a negative state is often fast, but it is harder to exit it; being able to repair or reset during a fight is critical to stopping a spiral of escalating negativity.

- Husbands accepting influence from their wives, even if they did not agree with the wife's perspective. Comments such as, "I'll have to think about that" or "You make a good point" are examples.

- Wives raising concerns with a *soft start-up* at the outset of a conflict that did not make their partners immediately defensive, such as, "When you cleaned up your clothes yesterday, I felt that you'd been listening to me, but today I was upset to come home to last night's dishes."

- The presence of humor during a conflict. The caveat here is that there is a fine line between good-natured humor and hurtful sarcasm. When fighting includes the latter, it can exacerbate the conflict.

Fights are part of the bargain of being in an intimate relationship. The goal is not to eradicate conflict, but to make arguments less corrosive to the health of the relationship by paying attention to *how* couples are fighting. Most basically, therapists should help couples avoid patterns that escalate the conflict and focus instead on including statements and non-verbal behaviors that bring in positive affect during a fight.

Questions About *Relational Dilemmas*

- "What is your mutual understanding about fidelity? What are the rules going to be? Are you going to allow sexual encounters outside of the marriage? Online only? Are you going to be free to have sex with another person when traveling? Do you have an agreement that you can bring home a third person?

Do you want to know or not whether your partner has sex with someone else? What are your motivations for an open relationship?"

- "What are your fights like? Do they ever become physical with pushing, shoving, slapping, throwing objects, punching walls? Has your partner insisted on sex even when you did not want it? Have either of you threatened to hit or harm the other or yourself? Do fights become physical when either of you has been drinking or using other substances? Have either of you needed to see a doctor because of a fight with your partner? If you have answered *yes* to any of these questions, we can proceed in couple therapy only with a solid no-violence contract and with each of you also agreeing to individual therapy."

- "Would you re-enact a disagreement that you have at home? Then, I could give you feedback about how you are fighting, in terms of the presence or absence of the Four Horsemen, your use of repair statements, and whether you make positive comments to one another."

Protective Factors to Include in Therapy

Helping Couples Create Their Own Rituals

Creating rituals—the repeated sequence of actions that also offer shared meaning, identity, and a sense of belonging—is a comforting and vital practice for couples. When a clinician asks about a couple's dinner rituals, for example, the couple gets a chance to tackle one of the main tasks of this stage: figuring out what they want to carry forward from their families of origin, and then deciding how to combine and invent new practices that suit their unique relationship. The therapist may begin with exploration of their childhood dinners, which is a pipeline into their childhoods (Fishel, 2015; 2016). One person might describe a boisterous scene filled with political arguments and everyone free to interrupt one another. The other member of the couple might recount memories of dinners where family members ate as quickly as possible with little conversation, except for parents correcting table manners.

When two people put their very different snapshots of childhood family dinners side by side, they can engage in the process of making decisions together that were previously made separately or by their families. While there are lots of things to figure out—how to fight, spend or save money, make friends, use time, choose a place to live—developing a dinner ritual is a one place to start creating their own new family.

- "What was dinner like in your family growing up?"
- "What do you remember about dinner conversations? What did you enjoy talking about? Was there anything that made you uncomfortable?"
- "What was the meaning of food? Was it about love, control, nurture, experimentation, or something else?"
- "Think about how your parents handled the division of work around dinner. Did the work fall to one person, or was it shared each night or in an alternating way? Did the work feel like a burden?"

Then, the couple can be asked to reflect on their own rituals:

- "Do you want to alternate the cooking and the cleaning up? Do you want to do some parts together, like the shopping and meal planning, but then divide up the food preparation and dish washing? Or, do you want to take turns, so that each person has an *on* night and an *off* night?"
- "Will you want to turn off phones and other electronic devices so as not to be distracted by work intrusions? Or, establish some other guidelines?"
- "Are there topics you particularly enjoy talking about at dinner? What makes you feel reconnected to each other after a day apart?"

These same questions can be adapted to ask about other rituals—bedtime, saying goodbye or hello when they part or reunite after work, or sex—that may be more compelling to a given couple.

Exploring the Positive

Negative interactions are a stronger risk factor than positive communications are protective in early marriage (Markman et al., 2010). Consequently, couple therapists need to work double-time to decrease destructive communication, as well as to promote the expression of warmth, tenderness, playfulness, admiration, sexuality, and support. One negative zinger may pack more of a punch than many endearments, which is why Gottman has found that positive comments must outweigh negative ones by a 5 to 1 ratio.

Given the powerful impact of negative comments, a vigorous pursuit of connection is needed as a counterweight. For starters, couple therapists should forthrightly ask about sex:

- "You have not mentioned your sexual relationship, and maybe that is because it is going well, or because it is hard to bring it up with a stranger, but I would like to know if that is an area you might want to talk about, once you feel more at ease with me."

The therapist may also want to ask directly about the couple's strengths and what they each admire and cherish in the other. This focus on what is going well and on what nourishes a couple is, of course, not specific to this early stage of development—it will be a current that runs through all of the stages.

- "What are three positive adjectives to describe your partner, and could you share an example of when your partner displayed this trait?" (Olson & Olson, 2000).
- "What are the ways that you feel connected to and cherished by the other, and are they the same for each of you or have you had to learn new ways of expressing love?"
- "What are some recent times when you have felt close and connected to one another? How do you go about inviting in and cultivating those times?"

The complexity and importance of this stage demand that the therapist pay attention to the potential risks and vulnerabilities for couples as manifested in their family-of-origin matters, issues of timing, and relational dilemmas. But, this is also a phase that holds enormous promise, with patterns of interaction still amenable to change, often before life stressors have taken their toll. When couples have a strong connection and a compelling origin story about their first attraction to one another, this stage is also one that can be drawn on for sustenance and built upon for rejuvenation during later points in a relationship.

CHAPTER 3

Transition to Parenthood

Expanding the Dyad

A good marriage is a risk factor for having children.
—Tom Bradbury, UCLA marital researcher

The transformation from being a childless couple to having a baby is the most exciting and stressful transition in the marital life cycle. Many researchers have found that about two-thirds of new parents experience a moderate to severe decline in marital quality during the first two years after the birth of a first child (Belsky & Rovine, 1990; Cowan & Cowan, 1999; Gottman & Gottman, 2007). When compared with childless couples, married a comparable number of years, couples with children under the age of two years experience more conflict and less marital satisfaction (Crohan, 1996; Doss et al., 2009; Schulz, Cowan, & Cowan, 2006).

A decline in marital happiness has been found even in countries that provide more generous parental benefits and leave policies than the United States (Kluwer, 2010). A similar decline is seen in White as well as African-American couples (Crohan, 1996), so the stressors of this transition cannot be attributed solely to sociocultural factors. These dips in relationship satisfaction are not inevitable, however, and we will also focus on what has been learned from those couples who maintain or even improve their relationship following the birth of a baby.

What Is So Stressful About This Transition?

By conservative estimates, care for an infant adds at least 35 hours of work per week (Craig & Bittman, 2005). This *increased workload* means that new parents spend most of their days and nights taking care of the baby or working outside of the home, but not spending time with each other

(Huston & Vangelisti, 1995). In addition, many of the self-care activities that each partner performed seamlessly and autonomously before becoming a parent must now be coordinated with the partner. This *increased interdependence* shows up in small interactions. One new mother pleads with her husband, "Will you hold the baby so that I can take a shower?" Or, "You got to work out yesterday, so today it's my turn," or "Who will get up with the baby tomorrow morning?"

Partly, because of fatigue, and also because couples have to make multiple decisions on the spot, couples with babies often experience an *uptick in conflict and fighting* (Cowan & Cowan, 1995,1999; Kluwer & Johnson, 2007). Couples also have less time available to resolve their fights, and so resentments may build. Time pressure, noise, getting behind in taking care of daily household chores, and lack of sleep also can contribute to a high level of irritability and difficulty controlling angry outbursts (Twenge, Campbell, & Foster, 2003).

Lack of time to spend alone together and overall exhaustion are largely to blame for the *decrease in sexual activity and sexual satisfaction* that has been observed in more than half of new parents (Cowan et al., 1999; Grote & Clark, 2001). Another contributing factor may be a decrease in sexual desire in nursing mothers, as well as pain during intercourse following childbirth. Men's psychological discomfort may also play a role. Some men feel strange engaging in intercourse when there is a "baby in there," and even once the baby is born, new fathers may find it challenging to view their wives as both sexual beings and as mothers. However, many couples experience a greater sense of intimacy and connection that arises from the shared passion of caring for their baby (Person, 1989; Petch & Halford, 2008).

The negotiation around time—who does what and is it fair and equitable?—is the number one fight that new parents have. In heterosexual couples, a very common version of this conflict arises from husbands' and wives' different expectations about how the workload will be shared. Women often expect that the division of labor will closely resemble the more egalitarian division that characterized their pre-baby household. However, one of the changes reported by several researchers is that the *division of labor becomes more gender-stereotyped and less egalitarian* after the baby is born. Men may feel that they are doing much more than their own fathers did, and so feel unappreciated for their contributions (Belsky et al., 1985; Goldberg & Perry-Jenkins, 2004). Women, on the other hand, may feel disappointed and resentful that their partners are not sharing the workload as equitably as they had expected. Women who anticipated that their husbands would share equally in childcare reported steeper declines in marital satisfaction (Belsky et al., 1985; Goldberg & Perry-Jenkins, 2004; Lawrence, Nylen, & Cobb, 2007). Conversely, women whose husbands participated more in childcare enjoyed better mental health and higher marital satisfaction (Gjeringen & Chaloner, 1994), and husbands' support in the initial period after the baby's birth was associated with less postpartum distress among women one year later (Stemp, Turner, & Noh, 1986).

Among same-sex couples, however, equitable child-rearing and domestic chores based on mutual agreement and on individual prefer-ence, rather than gender expectation, are more often the norm (Goldberg & Perry-Jenkins, 2007; Schacher, Auberbach, & Silverstein, 2005). When parenting is de-gendered, gay and lesbian parents are more likely to take turns in taking full- or part-time jobs to accommodate childcare. The freedom to choose a parenting role that fits one's preferences rather than one's gender can result in greater satisfaction for same-sex couples than their heterosexual counterparts (McPherson, 1993).

Some of the most profound changes occur as each member of the couple absorbs *internal changes* involved in becoming a parent.

A couple married five years with a six-month old came to therapy prompted by Hilary's complaint that her husband had changed in ways that were unrecognizable to her. Anthony had always been her steady North Star, while she described herself as moody and hot-tempered. After the birth of their son, Anthony felt tired, left out of the cozy nursing dyad of mother and son, and re-experiencing feelings of loss of his own father, who had died when he was 10 years old. For the first time in their relationship, he wanted comfort and reassurance. He brought sad and angry feelings to Hilary, rather than the other way around. When asked to come up with an image of their relation-ship, Anthony said that he was the interesting stuff in the foam at water's edge, while Hilary was a cat that approached the foam, but then ran away from it. Hilary pictured herself as a rabbit overlooking a calm, peaceful lake that was Anthony. When she wanted to enliven the lake, she would throw a stone or pull up a grass at water's edge. The couple quickly saw that Hilary's image conveyed their relationship before Ben's birth, while Anthony's was an image of them now. Therapy began by helping Hilary tolerate the unfamiliar affective mess at water's edge without running away and by encouraging Anthony to bring more of his emotional life to Hilary, so as to keep pace with the individual changes brought on by becoming a father.

In addition to these individual changes, the couple must create a new bond as parents. Some couples struggle to support each other, ask for help, appreciate the new aspects of their parenting identities, and acknowledge differences in beliefs about parenting carried forward from their own families. When partners have valued their autonomy, it may feel unnatural to have to ask for help when too tired to calm a fussy baby, or to negotiate with a partner for time to exercise or eat. The transition from partners to parents is also a chance to revisit differences between the two families of origin and to feel the echo of generational issues as they resonate with this shift in roles. For example, when both members of a couple grew up in families where their mothers stayed home, it may feel disloyal or at least unfamiliar to have both parents work outside the home. If the grandparents express disapproval, any conflict between the couple about their work choices will be intensified.

On top of all these stressors entailed in the transition to parenthood, there are additional ones that may challenge same-sex couples, couples who use assisted reproductive technology (ART) or adoption to become parents, and remarried couples whose new baby joins step-children from a previous relationship.

Same-Sex Parents

The confluence of increased rights allowing legal adoption for same-sex couples, as well as opportunities for family creation through IVF, has led to more lesbian and gay couples choosing parenthood, although there is only a relatively small body of research on same-sex couples' transition to parenthood (Cao et al., 2016). About 50 percent of lesbians and 20 percent of gay men are raising children, compared to about 70 percent of heterosexuals (Gates, 2015). While same-sex couples face many of the same challenges as heterosexual ones in the transition to parenthood, they may also experience additional strain by virtue of living in a heterosexist society (Cochran, Greer & Mays, 2003; Goldberg & Smith, 2008). Couples who can mitigate the effects of homophobia by living in welcoming neighborhoods, in states that are legally favorable to gay adoption, and in families that are supportive will experience less anxiety and depression (Goldberg & Smith, 2011). In one recent study of gay men who became fathers through gestational surrogacy, a striking finding was that fathers reported greater closeness with their families of origin and enhanced feelings of self-esteem as a result of having and raising children (Bergman et al., 2010). Many same-sex parents, however, will have to navigate changes to their relationship without the advantage of older role models who can offer guidance and support outside of a heteronormative model of the traditional family. Seeing a lesbian or gay therapist may be especially helpful during this stage of development, as he or she can serve as a witness and mentor, for a couple lacking both in their families of origin.[1]

ART-Facilitated Transition to Parenthood

With the advent of ART, there are additional issues for new parents, straight and gay. Couples who have conceived through egg sharing, artificial insemination, surrogacy, and in vitro fertilization (IVF) must make decisions about how to answer their young children's questions about how they became a family. The American Society of Reproductive Medicine (ASRM) advises parents who conceive through ART to tell children their birth stories by the time they are three years old, advice that mirrors that given to adoptive parents. Same-sex and different-sex parents who have used ART or adoption to create families may find it helpful to start scripting and telling their family stories to each other, so that by the time a child is old enough to understand and ask questions, the couple will be comfortable with the narrative of their shared story.

Michelle and Adelaide are a married biracial couple with two eight-month-old sons, conceived with co-IVF: Each woman used a donor egg and a friend's sperm, and then each mother carried an embryo. Since the eggs came from two different women and the sperm from the same man, the two children are half-siblings genetically and are functionally twins. The couple came for

---

[1] Caroline Marvin, PhD, personal communication, March 24, 2017.

help with increased conflict around their parenting differences, conflict that was a new and unwelcome aspect of their relationship. One recurring fight was around nursing. Adelaide wanted to nurse for longer than Michelle, but did not want Michelle to feel judged as a mother for switching to bottles, nor did Adelaide want to feel judged for her choice. Michelle explained that she wanted Adelaide to stop nursing so that they would have more time to spend together and with their children. In an attempt to avoid conflict, Adelaide tried to nurse Alex when she thought Michelle was not paying attention, but this strategy often backfired. When Michelle found Adelaide nursing, she accused her of being sneaky and secretive. They came to understand these tensions around nursing as reflective of the competition they felt about being two mothers, where neither one wanted to defer to the other, but each felt like an expert. They joked that it would be easier if one of them were a man, because then he would have to defer about breastfeeding and other parenting decisions.

In addition to wanting help understanding and defusing their fights, they also wanted to figure out how and when to tell their children's birth stories to their families and to their sons. They were no strangers to complex family constellations. A Caucasian family with one biological son adopted Michelle at birth from Korea, while Adelaide had grown up in a Caucasian family with half-siblings from her mother's first marriage. Michelle felt that she and her brother had been treated the same and downplayed the significance of genetic connection as an important factor in family bonding, but Adelaide drew different lessons from her childhood experience. Her father had refused to adopt Adelaide's mother's two children from a previous marriage (that ended in the death of the husband), because they were not his genetically. Despite her father's differential treatment of the two sets of siblings, Adelaide reported that all of the siblings felt close to one another.

In therapy, the couple began to co-create a family story that wove together these two powerful legacies: "Our family is part of a patchwork quilt that has many different squares, portraying different ways of how children come to belong to a family. I'll tell you about our square. When we got married, we knew we wanted to have children and we set out to find a way to make that happen." They then told the stories of how they chose their egg donors, the conversation they had with their friend who offered his sperm, their excitement at learning they were pregnant, and their surprise that they were due at the same time. The story is also a tale of perseverance and courage, as they each endured multiple rounds of IVF. Adelaide and Michelle will tell and retell this story to each other, modifying it, and adding new facts and feelings as they recount it. Over time, they will decide which version to tell their families, and what to tell their sons, but they will be ready well before Alex and Sam turn three.

Step-Families Making Transition to Parenthood

When there are already children from previous relationships, the transition to parenthood entails additional challenges for the remarried couple, and half of all remarried couples will eventually have a child together (Pasley & Lee, 2010). Papernow (2013) explores the particular family *architecture* of step-families and offers layered, nuanced advice for families and clinicians about how to navigate step-family dilemmas involving parents' asymmetries and children's divided loyalties. The intense connection between the couple and their new baby may throw into bold relief how much less intimate the step-parent–step-child connection is. Step-children may feel sidelined by a new sibling, while parents may feel guilty that their new baby will be raised by two parents living together, whereas their other children are not. Most broadly, step-parents who go on to have their own child will not be able to replicate an idealized nuclear family, but will need to create more flexible relationships within the family and not rush step-children to bond with their new half-sibling. As a couple, they will need to discuss not only what they want to carry forward from their families of origin, but what they have learned from being parents with previous partners.

Clinical Questions and Interventions

Given the stress and seismic shifts that accompany the transition to parenthood, it is not surprising that, in recent years, 40 percent of all the couple's referrals made to a major teaching hospital are from couples with children under the age of four years.[2] What is unexpected, however, is that these couples rarely point to their young children or their status as new parents as the reasons for coming to therapy. Instead, they note that

---

[2] Fishel records of couples referrals made to Massachusetts General Hospital, 2015–2017, unpublished.

they are having the worst fights of their lives, or they have not had sex in a year, or they are feeling unloved and unappreciated. This paradox of couples experiencing high stress, without making mention of its likely cause, may be attributable to the cultural taboo about new parents grousing and a prohibition against feeling anything but positive emotions toward young children.

There is another paradox at the heart of this stage. Babies need safety, warmth, consistency, and well-attuned attention for developing secure attachment and brain development, but this time period coincides with a period of elevated stress for their parents, low levels of marital stability, and higher rates of depression and anxiety, not to mention common feelings of exhaustion and irritability. At the very time when babies need the most attention and care, their parents may be at their most depleted.

Taken together, these two paradoxes point to the importance of interventions and psychoeducation for couples that can help strengthen families during this exciting, if difficult, transition.

What Is Helpful to Expectant Parents?

Better Prenatal Marital Quality

Not surprisingly, couples who have less conflict and more positive interactions before becoming parents are less vulnerable to declines in their marital quality after a baby arrives (Curran, Hazen et al., 2005). In a longitudinal study of 130 newlywed couples, Gottman et al. (1998) found that certain characteristics early in marriage predicted a happier transition to parenthood: Husbands and wives expressed a heightened awareness of the other's inner world and knowledge about their work and friendships; husbands had a higher level of fondness and admiration toward their wives; and both members of the couple felt some control over important events in their lives. Certainly, when clinicians are working with couples who are anticipating having a child, they should focus on strengthening the couple's positive interactions and their knowledge of each other's worlds.

Discuss Expectations Around the Couple's Relationship

Several researchers have noted that couples do better when they are less disappointed and blind-sided by the changes wrought by new parenthood.

For example, couples who earned lower romance than friendship scores prenatally did better during the transition to parenthood (Belsky et al., 1990). Perhaps, couples who valued their friendship with one another were less dissatisfied by the common decline in sexual activity that often accompanies this stage.

Couples who have witnessed marital distress in their own parents may counter-intuitively have an advantage in the transition to parenthood. When couples were asked to tell stories about the quality of their own parents' marriage, those who remembered their parents' marriage as being characterized by high conflict, little affection, and low levels of communication but who were also insightful about these memories had the greatest emotional attunement to their partners in the transition to parenthood. Most surprisingly, these couples did even better than those with purely positive memories of their parents' marriages and good insight (Curran et al., 2006). Perhaps, those who were able to anticipate marital difficulties, informed by some experience with negative interactions, were better equipped to deal with the inevitable distress of early parenthood. Therapists may want to ask questions that help couples anticipate some of the challenges to their relationship:

- "What do you think will be the most challenging change to your relationship once you become parents?"
- "What did you learn by observing your parents' marriages or by talking to them about difficult times in their marriages, about what helps and what aggravates these times?"
- "What are your strengths now, as a couple, that will help you if your sexual relationship diminishes after the baby is born, or if you experience more conflict with one another?"

Visualize and Discuss Fantasies and Expectations About Parenting

It can be very helpful for expectant parents to anticipate and imagine their new roles before fully inhabiting them. When couples carve out the time and space to visualize themselves as future parents, the actual transition goes more smoothly. Therapy can be a place to invite couples to imagine what they will enjoy and find challenging about becoming parents, how they will balance work and family obligations, and what some of their beliefs are about parenting.

The couple therapist might suggest that the rosy cast promulgated by the cultural discourse about the transition to parenthood does not offer the best preparation for making the transition to parenthood. Instead, it is important to anticipate what about caring for a baby, and about their relationship as a couple and as parents, may be difficult in this transition. For example, women who expected their babies' temperament to be easier and who expected to find parenting a mostly positive experience reported steeper declines in their marital satisfaction.

In addition, couples can explore some of their beliefs about parenting that derive from their experiences in their own childhoods. For example, "Do you think that babies should always be responded to when they cry?" or "Do you think that a child should be able to question the authority of his or her parents?" Or, "Does too much attention to a baby result in spoiling?" Therapists may want to weave in some parent psychoeducation here, such as the truism that it is impossible to spoil a newborn.

Some of this conversation can be aimed at surfacing their expectations of parenting to see where there are discrepancies or misunderstandings between the two partners. A helpful tool is the Cowans' Pie, which consists of a single sheet with a large circle and the instruction to each member of the couple to "make a list of the main roles that make up your life right now, for example, partner, artist, father, daughter, teacher, lover." Then, clients are instructed to divide the pie into pieces so that "the whole pie is a picture of you as your life is right now, where each pie slice corresponds to with how large that part feels to you." Subsequently, each member completes the exercise again, but this time making the pie slices correspond "to the way you'd like your roles to be" (Cowan & Cowan, 1990). Members of the couple can compare their pies in an effort to understand each other's self-perceptions and expectations for parenting.

When couples adopt a child or conceive with the aid of ART, they often refrain from fantasizing or planning their future roles as parents. In one study of couples who had conceived with IVF, most reported that they held off preparing the baby's room, talking about themselves as parents, and fantasizing about their baby (Fishel, 2011). As one expectant parent explained, "We haven't discussed future changes in work or home roles yet because of the fear of having a miscarriage." Others noted that they had been planning their pregnancy from one medical appointment to another and felt that they would be inviting bad luck to dare to imagine themselves as parents (Fishel, 2011). Given that anticipating the future is a predictor of positive adjustment to parenthood, clinicians should encourage couples who might otherwise be reluctant to fantasize and imagine their lives with a baby.

Mobilize Support

It is useful to ask couples to discuss what kind of help, if any, they will want from their own parents and families, and whether they have any plans for getting extra support with cooking, cleaning, or helping with the baby. There can often be discrepant points of view between how the future grandparents imagine their involvement and what the new parents want. Therapy can be a place to clarify those disjunctions and figure out how to let parents know that they will not be welcome in the delivery room, or that their cooking meals for the first few weeks would be a great gift.

In general, families with fewer financial resources and less support from family or from paid help will encounter more challenges. A shorter maternity leave (fewer than 12 weeks) is associated with more maternal depression and marital distress (Feldman, Sussman, & Zigler, 2004). Given that the United States is the only industrialized country that does not provide universal paid leave for new mothers, many families, particularly those with limited financial reserves, will have a hard time eking out a three-month break from work. In addition, working non-day shifts, often to avoid high-cost childcare, is correlated with depressive symptoms and marital conflict during the first year of parenthood (Perry-Jenkins et al., 2007). Working overtime, usually by men, is a common flash point for marital arguments (Kluwer, Heesink, & Van de Vliert, 1996). If a new father is able to take paternity leave and stay home for a few weeks with his partner, that time will be extremely salutary in promoting bonding and in easing the transition back to work.

Offer Time to Express Concerns About Labor and Delivery

While most parents will prepare for delivery by participating in childbirth classes, couple therapists can and should inquire about the couple's fears and needs concerning delivery, as these will typically not be covered in classes. If there are tragic childbirth stories in their family histories, such as stillbirths or maternal deaths, the couple may carry an extra burden of anxiety. In addition, couples who have undergone infertility treatment, had difficulty conceiving, or had previous abortions may also have additional concerns about childbirth.

While some first-time parents who conceive using IVF experience a heightened anxiety about becoming parents, many also report feeling that their relationship improved after infertility treatment (Holter et al., 2006; Lieblum et al., 1998). As one woman put it, "In some ways infertility strengthened our relationship. Before that, our life was a fairytale. Infertility was our first real challenge, and we've grown together" (Fishel et al., 2011). Couples who have endured multiple rounds of IVF, who have experienced pregnancy loss, or have searched for surrogates, egg, or sperm donors may benefit from the opportunity to tell their stories, integrating the medical and emotional aspects. Therapy is often the first and only place where couples have a chance to tell this story, and in the process, feel an increased sense of resilience and connectedness that can ease the transition to parenthood.

Discuss Postpartum Depression in Men and Women

Maternal and paternal depression have a major effect on the couple's relationship and on the baby's early brain and emotional development. It is estimated that 12 percent of all pregnant or postpartum women experience a clinical depression, and for low-income women the prevalence is doubled (Earls, 2010). Paternal depression is estimated at 6 percent and may be higher if the mother is also depressed (Goodman, 2004; Isaacs, 2006). A family or personal history of depression, lack of social support, and stressful life events increase the risk of perinatal and postpartum depression. As there can be stigma for new parents to admit that parenting is overwhelming and difficult, asking screening questions of both men and women about depression is important. Couples can also be reassured that early intervention through medication or therapy is very effective for postpartum depression.

What Is Helpful to New Parents

Normalize Increase in Fighting, Decrease in Sex

Sharing the knowledge that most first-time parents will fight more and have sex less can lower a couple's feelings of blame and distress. Some couples can participate in couples' groups where they will learn that other couples share many of their same challenges (Cowan & Cowan, 1999; Feinberg, Kan, & Goslin, 2009; Gottman & Gottman, 2007). Alternatively, they can read books that normalize common experiences of early parenthood. *And Baby Makes Three* (Gottman & Gottman, 2007) and *When Partners Become Parents* (Cowan & Cowan, 1999) are excellent guides for parents as they anticipate normative challenges such as increased marital fighting, decreased sexual activity, and marital dissatisfaction. Couple therapists can embed common challenges into their questions:

- "A majority of couples experience a decrease in their sexual activity in the first few years after a baby's birth. How is this going for you?"
- "Most couples are surprised to find that they are much more irritable with one another during the postpartum period. You have to negotiate so many issues on the spot about your baby and your time, and all this on much less sleep. Have you noticed any increase in conflict?"
- "Most couples find that they are organizing the childcare and household work in a more gender-traditional way than they did before having children. Is this true for you?"

Create New Rituals for the Couple

Most new parents are starved for time to spend with each other but may not have the money to pay a babysitter or may feel guilty putting their needs ahead of spending time with their baby. It is worth offering the perspective that the parenting relationship flows directly from how robust the couple's relationship is, so that time spent tending to the relationship is good for the baby too. Couples need time to discuss all the changes that have shaken their lives—from the inner changes that accompany becoming a parent to their new relationships with their families of origin, from changes in their sexual relationship to their jobs. Couples can be encouraged to make time at home by putting their baby to sleep, turning off phones and other devices, and making a plan to do something together, like cooking and having dinner, making a special dessert, watching a movie, or having sex. Helping a couple create a new ritual that gives them a predictable event to look forward to, apart from their new responsibilities as parents, is protective of their relationship. A therapist can explore the topic of time and rituals:

- "How do you make room for each other, now that so much energy and time is directed toward caring for your child?"
- "How do you continue to keep up with the important aspects of your partner's life? Do you discuss the ways that you have changed since becoming a parent?"
- "If you were to create a new ritual for you as a couple, where and when do you think it should take place? How will you make it feel different from the rest of your week? Is there music, clothing, food you want to include? Will you share the planning or take turns? What feelings will be important in this this ritual—for example, relaxation, gratitude, celebration, renewal, sexual connection, or something else?"

Practice Repair, Gentle Startup

Because increased conflict is an expected byproduct of the transition to parenthood, therapists can invoke some of Gottman's techniques to minimize the toxicity of fighting. In particular, couples can be encouraged to make repair statements, such as "My reactions were a bit too extreme, sorry, let me try again," or "I'm getting worried, scared or sad." In addition, therapists can underscore the importance of positive comments or nonverbal gestures made during a fight. Requests for change can be softened by preceding appreciative statements such as "It felt so good to me that you made dinner tonight, it was delicious. I also wondered if we could turn off our phones during dinner so that can really focus on each other." Therapists can also point out occurrences of these positive moments during conflicts that take place in the therapy office, so that couples will be more mindful of making them at home. Teaching the benefits of soft startup and accepting influence, as well as educating couples about the negative impact of defensiveness, stonewalling, blame, and contempt can diminish the spiraling downward effects of early parenthood fights (Gottman, 1999; Gottman & Silver, 2016).

Pay Attention to Dominant Cultural Stories That May Be Damaging or Constricting

The interplay of culture and parenting complicates the experience of becoming parents. Many commonly held stories about parenting can be mistaken for *reality*. For example, many women believe that they will fall in love with their babies in the delivery room, and that if they do not, there is something terribly wrong. Other parents may think that parenting is totally intuitive, and therefore does not require help from other parents, books, or relatives. Or, that babies who bottle-feed are inferior to those who nurse. Another cultural notion is that a good mother stays home with her baby, and in contradiction with that idea is another: that a stay-at-home mother is not pulling her weight because she is not earning money. Identifying and then dispelling such constricting myths can be helpful to new parents.

For same-sex couples, there may be fears that their baby is disadvantaged by not having a parent of the opposite gender. Therapists should share the growing body of research that shows that children's psychosocial adjustment is determined by the positive quality of the couple's relationship, rather than by a particular family structure (Gartrell et al., 2000; Goldberg, 2010; Golombok et al., 2014; Patterson, 2006). In other words, lack of serious parental conflict and the presence of a warm, supportive family atmosphere are the most important ingredients in raising happy, well-adjusted children. Moreover, there are advantages to children raised by same-sex parents: Children of both male and female same-sex parents exhibit less sex-typed behavior than children raised by heterosexual couples.

A couple therapist can try to dispel some of the constricting notions about parenting by asking:

- "What are the restrictive cultural stories that you have heard about the transition to parenthood?"
- "How do you try to resist some of these stories and leave room for your own?"
- "Some same-sex parents will expand the definitions of traditional caregiving roles by sharing both typically masculine and feminine behaviors (Benson, Silverstein, & Auerbach, 2005; Goldberg, Kashy, & Smith, 2012). How do you stretch the meaning of gender roles in your relationship?"

Discuss Infants' Temperament; Address Sleeping Challenges

While parents have little control over the ease with which a baby sleeps or eats, a baby's temperament is a major variable in predicting a couple's marital satisfaction in the transition to parenthood (Belsky, 1990). When a baby is awake every two hours throughout the night, it is unlikely that the parents will have the stamina to resume a sexual relationship. When a baby will not take a bottle, the father may struggle with feeling left out of the new mother–baby dyad. Parents whose babies sleep through the night and nurse or feed from a bottle with gusto will have a higher baseline of ease and confidence than parents whose babies are cranky, colicky, or less easy to soothe. A therapist might ask the following questions about the baby's temperament:

- "How is the nursing or feeding going?"
- "How many hours in a row does your baby sleep? What have you tried to lengthen that stretch? How has that gone?"
- "What do you do to soothe your baby when he or she is crying or fussy? How does your baby respond to your soothing efforts?"

Explore Their New Relationship as Parents

Co-parenting is different from having a marital relationship, and yet, most couples have not had a chance to discuss this new component.

When couples can integrate a sense of their shared identity as parents, they have an easier time in the transition to parenthood. Conversely, when one parent is not on board with the decision to become a parent, divorce is much more likely (Cowan, 1999).

Therapists can ask:

- "What has been most surprising about the other's new role as a mother or father? What do you appreciate about these new aspects?"
- "What do you like most and find most difficult about your new roles as parents?"
- "How do you see your parenting style as different from or similar to your partner's way of being a parent?"
- "Have you and your partner had any differences in opinion about childrearing issues?"
- "How do you ask for help from the other when you are feeling overwhelmed?"
- "How do you get and give support to the other?"
- "How do you each comfort, soothe, and play with the baby? Do you each feed the baby, put him or her to sleep? Does the baby seem delighted to see each of you? How do you help each other parent your baby?"

Couple therapists can play a major role in supporting new parents, both in their expectant and postpartum states. Questions and interventions that emphasize the normative challenges of becoming parents help couples develop the perspective that they do not have to blame each other for such common problems as an increase in fighting or a decrease in sexual frequency. This is a stage of life when the round-the-clock demands of caring for the many physical and psychological needs of a baby can easily deplete the energies of their fatigued, inexperienced, bewildered new parents. By focusing on the couple's strengths as new parents and their discoveries of each other and themselves as parents, therapy can help new mothers and fathers find the strength to traverse this seismic shift in their lives.

CHAPTER 4

Midlife Couples

Increasing Demands of Work, Parenting, and Care-giving

Thoroughly unprepared we take the step into the afternoon of life. Worse still, we take this step with the false presupposition that our truths and ideals will serve us as hitherto. But, we cannot live the afternoon of life according to the program of life's morning, for what was great in the morning will be little at evening and what in the morning was true, at evening will have become a lie.

—C.G. Jung, *Modern Man in Search of a Soul*

Compared to earlier stages, there is more variation in life paths as couples move into midlife, but there is less research to guide clinicians, particularly regarding couples who are other than heterosexual, middle-class White Americans (Bradbury & Karney, 2004). Even without a robust scientific literature, it is evident that social class, race, and sexual orientation continue to shape couple's relationships in midlife. For example, cohort differences may be more critical to lesbian, gay, bisexual, and transgender (LGBT) couples than to heterosexual ones, as current midlifers typically came out later than current LGBT youth. Gay people of color tend to disclose their sexual orientation later than their White American counterparts. One consequence of later identity formation is that earlier stages may bump up against midlife (Hostetler, 2013) so that the trajectories of LGBT couples do not follow the same course as heterosexual couples.

In a study that focused on midlife African-American married and cohabitating couples, income level and financial strain predicted relationship quality, a finding not highlighted in studies of primarily White couples (Cutrona et al., 2011). Fewer economic opportunities, racial discrimination, and minority stress likely have a cumulative impact on midlife marriages among couples of color, an impact that has not received much study.

I am defining midlife in this chapter as corresponding to a period in the life cycle when couples are aged 40 to 55, have children who are entering adolescence up until when the last one leaves home, or are in marriages of 15 to 25 years duration. But, to be in a midlife relationship, one does not need to hit all those marks. One can be a midlife couple who is married or cohabitating, raising an infant, sandwiched among four generations that includes parents and grandchildren, living with step-children, or in a relationship without children. And, there are many couples who expect that they are in the middle of their lives, but discover, instead, that impending death has telescoped many stages all at once. The midpoint of life is hard to pinpoint, after all, except retrospectively.

Most broadly, midlife is a time when many people take stock of their decisions thus far in life, increasingly mindful that time is finite and diminishing. They may ask themselves whether they want their lives to continue on the same path, or wish instead to make a course correction. Midlife often coincides with couples facing losses of one kind or another, sometimes for the first time—the loss of a job, a move to a new country or city, the death of a parent or close friend, the slowing of sexual vitality, and the awareness of other physical changes associated with aging. It is a time of life requiring large amounts of energy invested in taking care of children, often of aging parents too, and all while in the thick of maintaining work responsibilities. A couple's relationship, taking the back seat to all this activity and generativity, may suffer the consequences of neglect.

Midlife couples are not only in the midpoint of their lives, but also in the middle of their own family systems. Like their adolescent children who are renegotiating their relationships with parents to push for more freedom, midlife parents are also resetting their expectations of their own aging parents. The pendulum starts to swing, as the middle generation assumes more caretaking, such as hosting holidays or accompanying parents to their doctors' visits. Conflict between parents and grandparents can aggravate marital issues, as when one spouse feels that his or her partner's focus on an aging parent is detracting from caretaking on the home front. Additionally, stress between parent and adolescents may force changes upward, as when a grandparent wants more information about a grandchild's sexual orientation or mental health issues than an adolescent wants to provide. There can be turmoil up and down the generational tree.

The Reciprocal Effects of Adolescent Children on Midlife Marriage

There are two developmentally-informed ways to consider the reciprocal influence of adolescents on their parents (Fishel, 1999). One view emphasizes the commonality between adolescents and their midlife parents, as both are facing similar issues, such as hormonal fluctuations, changing relationships with parents, and identity questions. Both adolescents and parents are asking, for example, "Will I choose to be the same person in the next stage of life as I have been in childhood (for the adolescent) or in early adulthood (for the middle-aged parent)?"

The other view emphasizes that the two generations are working at cross-purposes and are generating inevitable conflict. For starters, the sexual drives of adolescents are on the rise, while their middle-aged parents' energies and libidos are waning. Furthermore, the two generations' sense of time and mortality are also at odds with one another. Adolescents see their futures as open-ended, while their parents are grappling with signs of mortality as they face their parents' aging and their own realization of limited time. Teenagers may dream expansively, whereas parents are dealing with the gap between their younger aspirations and the diminishing likelihood of achieving all those life goals. Although the notion of adolescents and their parents being locked in a battle with one another is a popular meme in TV shows, films, and novels, scientific studies indicate that heated, protracted conflict is not normative. Instead, when nonclinical adolescents are studied, researchers report that most adolescents emulate their parents' values and want to spend time with them. Reports of inevitable generational conflict are greatly exaggerated.

Another popular cultural idea, also unsubstantiated by research, is the phenomenon of a predictable midlife crisis. Instead, only about 10 to 25 percent of midlifers report experiencing a midlife crisis (Brim 1992; Wethington, 2000), while early adulthood and adolescence are actually the times of life most associated with dramatic turning points (Clausen, 1995). In 1965, Eliot Jacques coined the term "midlife crisis" as a time when individuals started thinking about death. Perhaps, as life trajectories have extended and as childbearing and marriage have been postponed, this term may be outdated.

If generational conflict and midlife crises are more cultural notions than scientific fact, two other phenomena do have scientific merit: Many parents experience increased distress when their children enter puberty and when their adolescents are on the verge of leaving home. The beginning of puberty can send shock waves through a family system. Over the course of a summer, a voice change, the arrival of facial hair, and a rapid growth spurt can transform a baby-faced 12-year-old boy into a gruff teenager, who towers over his parents and needs a razor. A parent may feel sad, or confused, by the change from having a child who easily shared confidences to one who now grunts out one-word responses. A father who was once easily affectionate may suddenly feel awkward around his pubescent daughter.

Parents report greater stress when their children are young adolescents than when they are preadolescent or middle-adolescent children (Small, 1983), largely because they must adjust to the dramatic physical changes brought on by puberty, feel less competent in the face of intensified conflict, and grapple with rejection when their adolescents demonstrate increased autonomy (Small, 1983; Steinberg & Silk, 2012). Even those parents who manage to retain a feeling of closeness with their young teens are not inured from some unwelcome change, as they may also report feeling more distant from their partners (Papini & Roggman, 1993).

The period leading up to children leaving home is also a simmering point for many midlife couples. Adolescents, ambivalent about being on their own, often intensify their conflict with parents, in part to ease the transition out of the home. Additionally, the pre-launching stage is a time of taking stock, when parents look back on their parenting, sometimes with regrets or with anxiety and disappointment about their children's future options. Parents may worry that they have not prepared their child adequately to cope independently and may even blame a spouse for perceived parenting deficits.

Several researchers have studied large samples to describe and explore midlife marriages. One sizeable, nationally representative study, Midlife in the United States (MIDUS), compared midlife couples to those younger and older (Brim, Ryff, & Kessler, 2004). Researchers found that, by midlife, only 5 percent of men and women had not tried marriage at least once, and that most midlifers had children (Marks, Bumpass, & Jun, 2004). By midlife, 20 percent of women and 25 percent of men are remarried. Physical health ratings take a downturn at midlife, and women's mental health dips below men's, especially when a woman is a parent to a child under the age of five.

Researchers found that midlife is a time of heightened engagement and responsibility both at home and at work. These two contexts require more demands on couples and have more impact on individuals' well-being during the midlife years than either before or after (Mroczek & Almeida, 2004). Given the salience of family and work, it is not surprising that the two biggest predictors of overall quality of life are one's marriage (or close relationship) and one's financial stability. In general, midlifers experienced higher levels of positive affect and lower levels of negative affect than younger couples. Those with higher levels of education also had higher levels of stress, most likely because of their job responsibilities, but experienced lower levels of negative affect than those with less education. Overall, adults' emotions, both negative and positive, were more affected by context (family and work) than it was for younger and older individuals.

While many midlife couples are caring for their aging parents, more than a quarter have lost both parents. Only 10 percent of men and 13 percent of women reported having both parents alive and healthy. Of the remaining respondents, another third had at least one unhealthy parent, and 20 percent had one sole parent in poor health. Of all the possible constellations, women who had a sole-surviving mother reported significantly higher rates of dysphoria.

In another large study of midlife, The Study of Marital Instability over the Life Course (Proulx & Snyder-Rivas, 2013), researchers found that marital happiness declined steadily over the life course. The news was not all bleak, however. Those couples whose decision-making became more equitable over time experienced an upward marital happiness trajectory. Older studies have reported a U-shaped curve, defined by marital satisfaction high at the start of marriage, then dipping when children are born, and rising again in the post-parental years (Glenn, 1989; Levenson, Carstensen, & Gottman, 1993). The older studies used cross-sectional rather than pooled-time series methods. Perhaps, the reported upswing in marital happiness later in life is a byproduct of unhappy couples being weeded out through divorce by their 60s and beyond.

While these previous studies included couples of color in their sampling, the National Survey of American Life (NSAL) concentrated on interviews of African-Americans and Caribbean Blacks. As with studies of primarily White couples, this research found that African-American women reported lower levels of marital satisfaction than did their male counterparts, suggesting that men received more benefits from marriage than do women. Among Caribbean Blacks, couples who had been married longest and had emigrated many years prior enjoyed the highest marital satisfaction. Another finding of the study was that difficulty with finances, around issues of budgeting, credit and debt management, was a key issue generating conflict and in turn, lowering marital satisfaction (Bryant et al., 2008).

Racial and ethnic differences were also found regarding whom couples turned to for support and to whom they offered their help. For example, African-American and Caribbean Blacks had much larger fictive kin (close relationships unrelated by blood or marriage) and church member networks than did Whites. African-Americans gave assistance to family members more often than did Whites and were more likely to have daily contact with extended family than did Whites or Caribbean Blacks. These racial differences suggest that a couple therapist needs to expand the definition of family, to include fictive kin and church family members when doing a genogram or asking about family supports.

Common Presentations

Reevaluation of marriage at midpoint: Will the next chapter follow smoothly from the previous one?

Couple therapy often begins with a difference of opinion between the couple about just how much change is required. One partner may wish that the relationship proceed along the past and current trajectory, while the other feels the need for discontinuous change (Fishel, 1999).

With the Palmers, a Euro-American couple in their late 40s, Sam stated that there were only a few adjustments required to improve their marriage. He loved his wife dearly, knew he had to learn to control his temper better, and saw therapy as "a tune-up." Sally, however, demanded a complete overhaul, or else she told Sam that she would want to divorce him. She felt that she had squelched her own wish to work in order to raise their two children and felt controlled by her husband's temper. She insisted on a new direction to the marriage that would include room for her to speak up more and voice her opinions, expand their social life, and go back to work without sparking Sam's verbal abuse. Without these changes, she said she would leave the marriage. In couple therapy, Sally voiced her long-standing unhappiness with Sam. He felt blind-sided and hurt to learn that that they had been living two very different marriages. He struggled to listen to her complaints and disappointments without resorting to withdrawal or anger.

When a couple has divergent views about how much change is required in therapy, it often mirrors the normative pulls of midlife. At the crossroads or midpoint of one's life, are dramatic changes warranted, or is this a time to edit and revise a life basically left intact?

Back-Burnered Problems Now Move Forward

When caring for young children while also trying to provide financially, many couples find that other issues get pushed aside or merely tolerated. By midlife, some issues refuse to be swept under the carpet. A long-standing drinking problem, the persistent effects of childhood trauma, or recurrent onslaughts of depression or anxiety often demand attention at midlife. One of the goals of an evaluation of a midlife couple is to figure out whether individual therapy is required instead of, or in addition to, couple therapy.

For the Palmer couple, Sam's volatile temper, along with the sequelae of childhood abuse at the hands of a cruel and punitive step-father, threatened to derail their marriage. While Sally had always hated to be at the mercy of his tantrums and threats to leave her, she no longer was willing to put up with his abuse, now that their two children, ages 17 and 18, were almost launched. Sam agreed to pursue individual therapy to learn to manage his anger and to confront the demons of his childhood. When they returned to couple therapy after a year of Sam's individual therapy, he was able to share his vulnerability before it had transformed into anger. When Sally witnessed Sam's interrupting an outburst in order to tell her how wounded he felt when she had hurt his feelings, she felt her tenderness toward him start to return.

Grappling with Loss

Midlife is often accompanied by loss and by the anticipation of more loss. Loss presents itself in a variety of ways: feeling the diminishment of sexual vitality, as well as the decline of physical fitness; experiencing deaths and illnesses of friends; making room for the frailty and demise of one's parents; acknowledging that one's children are no longer solely dependent on their parents; and looking ahead to the departure of one's children. Most adults at this stage of life will not have two healthy parents, and about 25 percent of midlifers will have lost both parents (Marks et al., 2004). How couples support each other as they face their parents' aging can be a turning point in a relationship.

Samantha and Charles, a couple in their 40s with three young teens, came to therapy during Samantha's breast cancer diagnosis and treatment. While she felt deeply hurt that her husband continued to travel for work and rarely accompanied her during chemotherapy appointments, the more devastating blow came a few months after her treatment had ended when her father died unexpectedly. Charles, who had often felt criticized by his father-in-law, made little room for Samantha's grief. Instead, he became irritated when she wanted to reminisce about her father or express how much she missed him. It was Charles' callousness to her grief, not helped by his distance when she was sick, that led her to request a separation.

Clinical Questions and Interventions

If couples with young children experience the sharpest spike in divorce rates, midlife couples with adolescents are the next most likely to be at risk for breaking up (Gottman & Levensen, 2000). Researchers have identified financial matters, sexual issues, displeasure with closeness and connection, and parenting difficulties as the most common problems at midlife (Christensen & Miller, 2006; Henry & Miller, 2004; Lodge & Umberson, 2012).

Money Issues

While financial stress is challenging for couples of any age, it is particularly difficult at midlife when there are intense pressures to provide for children's present and future needs, as well as societal expectations to be at the height of one's earning capabilities. At earlier stages, a couple can look ahead and still imagine that they will achieve their dream of buying a house or paying off school loans, but at midlife, these aspirations cannot easily be postponed. If a spouse loses a job in middle age, it can shake up a marriage, particularly if there is uncertainty about landing a new one. It may also be disequilibrating when a stay-at-home parent decides to return to work and consequently expects more help at home with chores and childcare, or when a primary breadwinner wants to switch careers, particularly from a secure lucrative job to one that is more personally fulfilling but riskier financially.

For parents who are preparing for college expenses, there are additional pressures and questions. Should a house be mortgaged, or retirement funds raided? Should grandparents be asked to contribute, or children expected to shoulder heavy student loans? Couples' differing cultural backgrounds, childhood experiences with money, and a sense of obligation to older and younger generations may come into conflict when couples attempt to plan for the financial future of their children and themselves.

Some questions for midlife couples about money:

- "How do you talk about money? Do you experience conflicts when you talk about how to make future plans or discuss how to handle debt?"
- "Do you have different expectations regarding your obligations to your parents and to your children?"
- "If you are planning for college, how do you plan to pay for it? Have you discussed your financial situation with your adolescent? Are you in agreement about how and whether you will fund your child's tuition?"

Sexuality

Both men and women experience sexual changes at midlife: Men's testosterone and women's estrogen production decreases, and both genders may require more direct stimulation to the genitals to allow for arousal. But all change is not equal. Most women may continue to be multiply orgasmic at midlife, with little diminishment in their responsiveness, while men's first physiological response and refractory period typically take longer than at younger ages. In one study, the percentage of women reporting that achieving orgasm was difficult or impossible did not increase significantly with age from 45 to 65 (Huang et al., 2009).

Sexual desire, however, does decline with age for both men and women, although men's desire for sex is higher than it is for women during midlife. According to an AARP study, 76 percent of men aged 45 to 59 reported desire a few times per week, while among women, the comparable percentage was 36 percent (Delamater & Koepsel, 2015). In a more diverse population, however, female sexual desire received higher endorsements with more than half of women aged 45 to 54 reporting at least moderate sexual desire (Huang et al., 2009).

Other than age, the main predictor of sexual desire is the importance of sex to the individual. Whether or not couples continue to value sex as they age is influenced by many factors, particularly social and cultural ones. Seeing positive media portrayals of midlife sexuality and having health providers who inquire about their sexual health are two affirmative influences on a continued interest in being sexual (Delamater & Sill, 2005).

One important gender difference, related to sexual desire, often emerges at midlife for women, particularly among those over 40 who have been having sex with the same person for 15 years or longer. In several studies, researchers found that the sequence of sexual desire preceding arousal did not hold for almost half of the women studied (Basson, 2000; Brotto et al., 2010; Cawood & Bancroft, 1996). Rather, while these women did not report spontaneously occurring sexual desire, they did report being receptive to sex and experiencing desire after they became aroused. In other words, for many women at midlife, sexual desire is not the trigger for having sex. Instead, the spark may be the wish to feel close to the partner or to feel sexual, powerful, and desirable; once sexual activity is underway, desire follows. Educating couples about this common reversal of sequencing of desire and arousal in midlife women can be very helpful, as it can break down barriers to sexual activity. Instead of both members of the couple waiting for sexual desire to strike before engaging in sex, couples can feel free to engage in sexual activity in order to engender sexual desire. There is an apt French expression that translates as *the appetite is in the eating*. A person not initially hungry may discover an appetite after taking a few tasty bites. Mindful that sexuality is also a type of appetite, the therapist can ask these questions about libido:

- "What makes for an inviting, or appetizing sexual encounter?"
- "Are there conditions, such as a back rub, a bath, or a walk in the woods, that make you more receptive to having sex?"
- "What are other prompts for you to think about sex, other than having spontaneously occurring sexual feelings?"

And, these questions about arousal:

- "For post-menopausal women, the lack of estrogen may cause atrophic changes to the vagina and a significant decrease in lubrication, sometimes making intercourse painful. Is that ever a concern for you?"
- "For men, a decline in testosterone, the use of anti-hypertensive medications and or of certain anti-depressants, as well as suffering from certain diseases, such as diabetes, alcoholism, and cardiovascular ones, may interfere with getting and keeping an erection. Is that ever a concern for you? Does anything make it easier or more difficult?"

Individual Changes Left Out of the Marriage

Many couples find that they have been so focused on the intensity of parenting and their engagement with work that they have lost touch with one another by the time they arrive at midlife. It is not only that couples may have neglected to spend the time and effort needed to stay connected during these very intense years. Often, there are also inner changes that accompany the development of a more mature self. Profound individual change can be brought on by many normative events of midlife, such as a parent's death, a serious illness, a job change, or the existential shock of mortality.

Despite having lost touch with each other's individual changes, many couples discover that they can catch up. At midlife, mutual access to each other's interior life can revitalize a relationship that has grown distant or is straining from loss, aging, and the pressures of parenting adolescents. Couple therapy can help couples expand their conversations with one another to accommodate these inner transformations, and in so doing, reengage a pair who may not have kept each other abreast of their worlds, both inner and external. If a couple becomes curious about each other's inner life, this is an endless source of novelty, which can breathe life into a relationship that feels stale and stuck (Person, 1988).

- "Do you share your dreams with one another?"
- "Can you speak as though you are writing in a journal, where the listener offers no judgments or opinions?"
- "What conversations are you aware of excluding from the other? What would be risked or gained by bringing up these topics?"
- "Are there aspects of your personality that you would like to change or tinker with?"
- "Are there adventures, hobbies, friendships, travels that you might want to explore in the next decade?"
- "What parts of your relationship—for example, being sexually intimate, trying a new activity, changing some of the ways you parent, deciding who your friends are—might you want to talk with each other about to deepen, change, and expand your relationship?"

Parenting

Many couples come to therapy with complaints, anxieties, and contentious differences of opinions about their adolescent children. Unlike parents of young children, who seem reluctant to assign blame for their marital difficulties on their children, midlife parents feel freer to point to their adolescents as the source of their own marital distress. For many parents, having an adolescent can stir the pot: A child's burgeoning sexuality is a reminder of one's own aging body. A teenager's expansive future can trigger a parent to reflect on having limited time ahead. An adolescent's questioning of identity and search to be known as a burgeoning adult can introduce more conflict into a family.

Beyond these normative disturbances, some come to therapy for support in the face of an adolescent's mental or physical health issues, or because they need help negotiating multiple treators and schools for a child with learning disabilities. Adolescence is a time when severe mental illness and substance abuse often first present.

For couples who are trying to manage the diagnostic ambiguities of a first-break psychosis, or are trying to access mental health services where there are few available, or where mental illness is a new and frightening subject colored by stigma, couples may enter a prolonged state of distress, confusion, and isolation from their peers and family. Many parents will also face the astronomical financial demands of trying to find suitable hospitalizations or residential schools, sometimes not covered by insurance, and enter into legal battles with their school systems to demand appropriate placements. Jobs often hang in the balance as couples need to take time off to search for mental health services, attend doctor appointments, or provide a safe landing spot for a child who is teetering on the edge of hospitalization. Some marriages will buckle under the pressure of managing a mental health crisis. Others will cling to each other for support and comfort, only to falter once the crisis is over, finding that they are unable to pick up the pieces of their lives with one another. Still others will feel their bond strengthened, particularly if they have been able to garner support along the way from family, friends, or professionals.

When couples are coping with a child with mental or physical illness:

- "Often parents divide up the emotional labor around caring for an ill child where one parent is more hopeful and the other more pessimistic; one is more stoic and the other more vocal about being frightened and anxious. How do you two handle all the emotion that is stirred up right now?"
- "Who else knows about your child's difficulties? Family, close friends, therapists? If you have not told anyone, what has prevented you from getting support?"

- "In addition to coming to see me, is there some extra support you could get? For example, from individual therapists, or in the instance of a having a child with mental health issues, by joining the National Alliance on Mental Illness?"
- "What do you two do for and with each other that focuses on your relationship, and that keeps your child's illness at bay, even for a few minutes at a time?"

Anticipating an Adolescent's Leave-taking

As couples stand on the threshold of a relationship without children living at home, the givens of marriage are up for grabs. Division of labor, expenditure of time, and life meaning derived from parenting are all about to change. Therapy at this time can serve as a kind of improvisational theater where couples can be asked to imagine how they want to reconstruct their roles and relationships before committing to a scripted performance. As couples look ahead to their children having left home, gone to college, or begun their first jobs:

- "How would you like to be spending your weekends?"
- "Do you imagine that you will make changes to your work lives?"
- "What do you hope your sexual relationship will be like when the two of you are home alone?"
- "Are there changes you want to make in your friendships, leisure activities, and creative pursuits?"
- "How much time will you want to spend together, alone, or with others?"
- "What would you like your relationships with your children to be like as they become young adults?"

Dealing with Loss

Often the losses that occur during midlife and the anticipation of those that lie ahead sharpen a midlife question: What really matters to you and to us? Are we together on what about life is most meaningful as we anticipate our next chapter together?

- "Did you feel empathy from your partner as you experienced losses over the past few years?"
- "What did you want from your partner during this time? What did you want or try to provide your partner during the time of loss or illness?"
- "How has the loss of your parent, or the experience of facing a life-threatening illness changed you? Have you let your partner in on these changes? How has your partner responded to ways that these losses have altered you?"

The couple therapist can provide an opportunity for a midlife couple to mourn previous losses that may not have been granted enough time during the busy years of childrearing. The therapist can also provide the axis around which to help the couple pivot backwards to review their marriage up until now, update each other on individual changes made during the previous decade, and repair problems that went unattended; to examine the present with its intense focus on work and parenting; and look toward the future to decide whether a touch-up or an overhaul is required for the years that lie ahead.

CHAPTER 5

Late Midlife Couples

Launching Children, Heading for Retirement, Becoming Grandparents

Love seems the swiftest, but it is the slowest of all growths. No man or woman really knows what perfect love is until they have been married a quarter of a century.

Mark Twain, 1894

The stage of late middle age—that is, from the time when adults are in their mid-50s until about age 70—has grown in length and importance in recent decades. A century ago, when the average life span was under 50 years, the critical milestones of launching one's children and seeing them married, burying parents, becoming grandparents, and losing a spouse to death usually occurred within a couple of years. With longer life expectancy and later start-times for retirement, more couples are now logging three decades and more with one another, and others are starting new marriages. On average, the period that begins when the youngest child leaves home and ends with retirement is now the longest stage in the life cycle.

This stage can feel like a rush-hour bus ride with passengers getting on and off multiple times: Young adult children may get back on after stepping off, and spouses may leave before the end of the line. At some stops, adult children may find partners and have children, while at others, many middle-aged couples cohabitate, remarry, and start new families. At the exit door, children move out, grandparents die, partners divorce, and are widowed. Couples at late midlife may be part of a two-, three- or four-generation family, with caretaking responsibilities extending to the couple's parents, children, and grandchildren. Most individuals are still working but are anticipating their exit strategy, evaluating their options in light of financial and health constraints. In short, couples present varied scenarios at this stage, which requires flexibility and activity.

As with previous stages, this one is affected by gender, cohort, socioeconomic status, race, ethnicity, sexual orientation, as well as by the marital, parental, health, and employment status of each partner, so that making sweeping generalizations runs the risk of obscuring important differences among couples. Reviewing the contemporary research and appreciating cultural trends can help us understand this stage of development.

The Gray Divorce

By 2010, almost half of ever-married Americans had been divorced or separated by the time they reached their late 50s (Kennedy & Ruggles, 2014). From 1980 to 2008, the number of late-middle-age divorces doubled among men and tripled among women (Brown & Lin, 2012), and the 2000 divorce rate among couples married 30 years or more increased by 16 percent (Hagen & Devries, 2004). Such statistics have given rise to the descriptor "the gray divorce." This uptick in late-middle-age divorces may be attributable to couples postponing divorce until their children are fully launched, or it may be due to the pressures of maintaining a marriage for more decades than was previously the norm, thanks to longer life spans. Alternatively, the cohort of couples who are now divorcing are the same baby boomers who also divorced at higher rates in their 20s and 30s, so the rates of later marital instability may reflect second marriages (and divorces) of these baby boomers.

The Emptying of the Nest Has a Positive Impact on Marriage

Several studies reveal that parents experience higher levels of marital satisfaction after the children leave home, as compared to how they felt during childrearing and launching phases (Dennerstein, Dudley, & Guthrie, 2002; Gorschoff, John, & Helson, 2008; White & Edwards,

1990). This increase in relationship satisfaction likely derives from couples having more time to spend with each other and from their having fewer roles to juggle. The increase in marital satisfaction is particularly pronounced soon after children leave home, rather than many years after their departure (Gorschoff et al., 2008). Spouses who have frequent contact with their adult children are more likely to report high general life satisfaction (Bouchard & McNair, 2016).

Marital happiness depends in part on how well the couple feels their children are managing emerging adulthood. If their children are functioning independently, parents feel less anxious and freer to focus on their own relationship (Bouchard, 2017; Dennerstein et al., 2002). Attitudes toward nest-leaving are influenced by cultural expectations about autonomy. For example, South Asian midlife parents are more likely to report distress when their children leave home than are Chinese, Southern-European, or British-origin parents (Mitchell & Wister, 2015).

But, the Empty Nest Is Often Not So Empty

Another demographic shift affecting couples in late middle age is the sharp increase in adult children continuing to live at home or returning home after a temporary departure from an empty nest. A Pew Report (2013) found that about 40 percent of adults aged 18 to 24 were living at home, and about half had moved back home at least once or had never moved out. While it has been common in working-class families for young adults to stay home until they marry or to move back home as young marrieds with children, this boomerang trend has become more common in middle- and upper-middle-class families. This trend has been attributed to lengthened years of education, changes in the global economy, delayed age of marriage, and rising health care costs (Arnett & Fishel, 2013).

The presence of adult children in the home can be particularly challenging for remarried couples, as they may expect that adult children will be unaffected by the introduction of a step-parent, and therefore adjust easily to a new family configuration. This expectation is predicated on two assumptions: First, that young adults will be so grown up that they will not be upset by their parents' divorce. However, one recent study found that almost 50 percent of gray divorcees reported that their children were *upset, very upset,* or *unsupportive* of their parents' divorce (Jensen & Brown, 2015).

The second erroneous assumption that older step-parents may sub-scribe to is that young adults will be out of the house. But, with half of young adults still living with their parents, many step-parents may discover that they still need to make room for a child. The adult child may feel resentful of a new step-parent sharing the home, while the step-parent may feel impatient and critical when a young adult is still living at home (Papernow, 2013). A very common clash between a parent and step-parent of young adults is for the former to want to offer emotional, physical, and financial support, while the latter subscribes to the belief that adult children should be on their own (Papernow, 2017).

Sexual Functioning Is Still Important

A critical cultural shift has been away from the notion that aging strips couples of their sexuality and toward the reality that couples continue to engage in sexual activity in their 60s and beyond. It is not just youth-focused popular culture that has promulgated the idea that aging and sexuality are antithetical. Until recently, research has been complicit as well. Prior research has endorsed cultural norms by limiting the age range of the cohort studied. For example, a large-scale study of *adult sexual behavior in the United States* limited recruitment to participants under age 60 (Laumann, Paik, & Rosen, 1999).

More recent research has revealed that individuals in late middle age and beyond do not cease their interest or engagement in sex. In surveys of men and women between 40 and 70 years, most participants rated *having a satisfying sexual relationship* as important to their quality of life (AARP, 2010). Studies conducted in this century reveal that among couples aged 57 to 64 years, three-quarters continue to be sexually active (Lindau, Schumm, Laumann, Levinson, O'Muircheartaigh, & Waite, 2007).

Having a sexual partner and being in good physical health were the single biggest predictors of sexual activity in late middle age. In a study of 1,550 women and 1,455 men, aged 57 to 85 years, there was little increase in sexual problems with increasing age for women, and only some increase for a cohort of men with erectile and orgasm difficulties (Laumann, Das, & Waite, 2008). The strongest predictors of sexual problems in aging couples were poor physical or mental health, or stress within the relationship, rather than as a direct consequence of aging (Laumann et al., 2008; Huang et al., 2009). As far as the impact of physical health on sexual functioning, diabetes and hypertension are associated with sexual dysfunction in both men and women. Regarding mental health, increased anxiety is associated with lack of sexual interest in both women and men, and depression is associated with anorgasmia and erectile dysfunction in men. Researchers have found only small negative correlations between sexual desire and use of medications such as anticoagulants, anti-cholesterol drugs, and anti-hypertensives (Delamater & Sill, 2005).

There is inconsistency in reports about the impact of menopause on sexual activity, with some women reporting less-frequent activity and others no change. In one study, two-third of postmenopausal women experienced vaginal dryness and atrophy due to estrogen decline, but serious symptoms, such as painful intercourse, were uncommon (Krychman, 2007). Women perceive the implications of menopause in different ways. Some women are distressed by their lack of reproductive capacity; others feel liberated by release from worry about unwanted pregnancy. The individual's perspective may influence the degree to which menopause becomes an obstacle to an active sex life.

Many older people welcome the chance to talk about sex and discuss issues they had not talked about before (Gott & Hinchliff, 2003). When health professionals inquire with respectful interest and sensitivity, couples may feel that their sexuality is validated and worth pursuing. The couple therapist's inquiries, indicating that sexuality is an important part of a couple's relationship, can be a partial antidote to a culture that does not offer many portrayals of vital sexuality among older people.

The couple therapist needs to be mindful that asking about sex is not synonymous with asking about intercourse. In a large study of men and women, aged 57 to 85 years, researchers found that, among those who were sexually active, about half of each group reported at least one bothersome problem: among women, low desire (43 percent), difficulty with lubrication (39 percent), and inability to orgasm (34 percent); among men, erectile dysfunction (37 percent) (Lindau, Schumm, & Laumann, et al., 2007). It is important that sexual activity be defined as "any mutually voluntary activity with another person that involved sexual contact, whether or not intercourse or orgasm occurs," so the term refers to much more than vaginal penetration. Using this definition, frequency of sexual activity did not decrease substantially until age 74, even though more than half of couples reported the presence of at least one sexual problem (Lindau et al., 2007).

Becoming Grandparents

While grandparenthood can begin when couples are in their 30s and extend until past the 100-year mark, late middle age is the most common time for couples to begin this adventure. With longer life expectancy, couples can now expect to inhabit this role for 30 or more years. Grandparenthood allows couples to assume many different roles—conveyers of family traditions and stories, caregivers who can focus on fun and play rather than discipline, source of financial help, and essential babysitters. In fact, an estimated 60 percent of the grandparents provide regular childcare to their grandchildren (Fuller-Thomson & Minkler, 2001).

In America today, there are few clear rights or responsibilities that accompany grandparenthood, and adults have little control over the role, as they do not choose the timing, the number, or even the frequency of contact. Many grandparents feel burdened when asked to assume financial and caretaking responsibilities, or may worry that they do not have the stamina to help care for children if they suffer from poor health. Still, becoming a grandparent is usually regarded as a highly positive event that offers opportunities to be generative and to experience a new role at a time in one's life when the centrality of work and parenting is receding. The role is related to boosts in self-esteem and to fewer depressive symptoms (Reitzes & Mutran, 2004). Those who enjoy grandparenthood report feeling younger and hope to live longer (Kaufman & Elder, 2003). The experience of being grandparents is enhanced by sharing the experience with a partner (Taubman-Ben-Ari, Findler, & Shlomo, 2013). Still, becoming a grandparent is not an essential ingredient of life satisfaction: Adults without grandchildren have been found to be as satisfied with their lives as those with grandchildren (Bouchard & McNair, 2016).

Cohort Effects of LGBT Couples

There is very little research on the long-standing gay and lesbian relationships of couples in late middle age, and specifically how these long-term relationships have survived despite a culture that has been challenging and hostile. The cohort of LGBT adults who are currently in late middle age have faced enormous stigma and have lacked access to legalized marriage until recently. Many gay and lesbian individuals entered heterosexual marriages at a time when that was the only way to have a family (Quam, Whitford, Dziengel, & Knochel, 2010), sometimes not coming out until middle age. Other LGBT couples are experiencing same-sex marriage for the first time late in life.

A few recent studies have looked at the long-term relationships of LGBT couples and found that many had already considered themselves married, even without legal sanction (Quam et al., 2010). Overall, only about 50 percent of older adults in same-sex relationships have opted to marry (Goldsen et al., 2017). Some may feel that marriage is too heteronormative as an institution, with attendant misgivings about mainstreaming same-sex relationships to fit into a straight society (Lannutti, 2010). They may feel wary about creating a public record having grown up in a culture where same-sex relationships were pathologized. Others may find it unnecessary if they have already created legal documents for health-related decision-making and financial protection. Still, being partnered or married is protective of physical and mental health for older LGBT adults (Wight et al., 2012; Williams & Fredriksen-Goldsen, 2014) and is associated with lower levels of stigma and loneliness (Kim & Fredriksen-Goldsen, 2016). In one survey study of LGBT couples who resided in states with legalized same-sex marriage, couples who were legally married reported better quality of life and more economic resources than unmarried partnered couples (Goldsen, et al., 2017).

Common Presentations

Ending a Long, Difficult Marriage Once the Children Are Launched

Many couples arrive at this stage hanging on by their fingernails to a marriage of several decades duration. They may have tolerated infidelities, partner indifference, alcoholism, or high levels of conflict in order to provide their children with a two-parent family where everyone lives in the same home. Once the children are off to college, in their own apartments, or settled with a partner, late-middle-age couples may question their commitment to staying married.

Bert (62) and Ally (61) had been college sweethearts with a shared creative dream to make documentary films together. They arrived in couple therapy as a last-ditch effort, having already separated, after Ally discovered Bert's affair. Both Ally and Bert came from poor families, but after a decade of scraping and saving, they had started a film production company, a creative focus intended to supplant the need to have children. Ally, however, became pregnant unintentionally soon after they married, and Bert confessed that he had always hoped to have children. Ally found that she enjoyed being a mother, and in retrospect recalls that she did not relish working so closely with her husband, whom she found competitive and domineering.

Over the next few years, they had two more daughters, this time on purpose. After their second daughter was born, Ally stepped back from documentary filmmaking to be a full-time mother, and in the process, began nursing decades of resentment. Rather than building a life that was entwined around a shared creative pursuit, each partner went in a different direction: Ally took charge of the children, while Bert worked long days in the studio. They ran the family as a business, with each one in charge of a specific department. Both Ally and Bert had always considered themselves fiercely independent, so constructing two parallel tracks seemed to suit them. They recall feeling proud of having built a family and a successful company, accomplishments that had eluded both sets of their parents, who had divorced and struggled financially.

But, once the children finished college and started to marry and have families of their own, Bert and Ally felt that they were left with the shell of a marriage. They were lonely together and often roiled with anger. Their arrangement of having two separate domains did not hold. Ally wanted acknowledgement and gratitude from Bert for having sacrificed her ambitions, and she also wanted to rejoin the production company. Bert, however, no longer wanted to share what he considered his company; he found Ally highly volatile and worried that she was drinking too much. Rather than feeling grateful for how well Ally had taken care of their daughters, he felt bitter because he had not been an integral part of their development.

The couple's lack of any real connection with one another ultimately pre-vailed over their wish to maintain a family base for their children and grand-children. Deciding to divorce, they worked in therapy to understand how they had created a family system that seemed to suit their needs for independence and control, but ultimately left them estranged from one another. With some difficulty, they agreed to share with their daughters a truthful narrative about their marriage that did not throw either one under the bus, but honored their 36 years of marriage, and took responsibility for each one's role in its demise.

Conflicting Dreams About Retirement

As couples head for retirement, there are many opportunities for conflict and disappointment. Each partner may be on a very different timetable. If one partner, often the woman, took time off for childrearing, but is now engaged in a career, she may want to work longer than her husband, especially if he had been looking forward to retirement years as a time of release and freedom. Some couples arrive at retirement without the financial resources to stop working, or with health issues that tether them to home. For many couples, planning for retirement is a last chance to actualize a dream. When couples feel that earlier dreams did not work out as planned, this chapter can be particularly charged.

Stanley (66) and Jo (66) married right after high school graduation when Jo found herself pregnant. Raised in a working-class Boston neighborhood, Stanley had earned a basketball scholarship to college that he forfeited to sup-port his wife and new baby as a bartender. When they came to therapy, they were both working part-time, and spending many hours a week as caretak-ers in the center of a five-generational web of family. Jo's mother, who had Alzheimer's, was living with them; two of their children were struggling with substance-abuse issues; and one granddaughter was a single mother, raising a child recently diagnosed with autism. Jo and Stanley helped out daily with the care of this great-grandchild.

The problem that brought them into therapy was an irreconcilable clash about their imminent retirement. Stanley wanted to fulfill his dream of mov-ing to Florida where he could fish, relax, and live simply without having to continue to take care of others. Jo felt tied to her mother, children, grandchil-dren, and great-grandchild—all of whom still needed her and gave her life meaning. In therapy, we explored these two discrete choices, which the couple did not have the financial resources to bridge by dividing their time between two places.

I asked each to talk about the dream that was contained in his or her retirement plan while the other listened and asked questions that deepened, but did not challenge the spouse's wishes. This exercise took each of them back in time to their families of origin and to the deferred wishes that were still very much alive. For Jo, she had never felt well cared for by her parents, and the opportunity now to be important to so many family members was deeply gratifying. For Stanley, he had sacrificed the wish to live simply and on his own terms at too young an age when he became a father and husband and had given up a college education. Later, I asked them each to comment on what about the other's perspective resonated with their own, and finally, to talk about any doubts or uncertainties they had about their own plans for retirement. As it turned out, both Stanley and Jo yearned for freedom from their lifetime of obligations, and they both recognized that being stable care-takers for their family had brought great satisfaction to each of them. As each partner felt understood and less defensive, they moved toward talking about their shared dreams for the future, with reassurance offered to one another that no individual dream was worth sacrificing staying together. By the end of therapy, they had decided to stay put and continue to be the hub for their family. Stanley was very disappointed that his dream was deferred indefinitely, but Jo had promised that they would take more time to do things together "just for fun."

Difficulties with Launching Children

If the empty nest is a halcyon period for many couples, especially when parents feel happy about their autonomous children's wellbeing, the converse is true as well. That is, when children are launched but floun-dering, or if they boomerang home because they are having mental health issues, a toll is often exacted on the couple's relationship.

Jim (59) and Peggy (57) came to therapy with complaints that they were exhausted from caring for their 24-year-old son, Jake, who was living at home, following years of numerous psychiatric hospitalizations for suicide attempts and for angry outbursts that became violent enough to prompt calls to the police. Diagnosed with bipolar illness and a personality disorder, Jake had seen several therapists and tried a variety of medications. A history of childhood sexual abuse perpetrated by Jake's mother's elderly uncle was revealed during the most recent hospital stay, two years earlier. The family therapy that followed that revelation was particularly helpful to Jake, in combination with medication, DBT groups, and individual therapy. Now, he seemed to be doing better than he had since his teens, as marked by his holding down a part-time job at a local animal shelter, attending night school, and maintaining a stable mood without any angry or self-destructive incidents for more than a year.

Despite Jake's improvement, his parents were deeply unhappy with one another. During his most turbulent years, they were in such a state of constant emergency and so focused on keeping Jake safe that they had ignored the mounting tensions between them. Now, with a bit of a respite and without the daily thrum of adrenaline, they were experiencing the longstanding toll of caring for and worrying about Jake. On a daily basis, they argued about how much supervision and nurture Jake continued to need. Peggy believed that they should not leave him alone on the weekends nor go out to dinner. Jim felt that he had already sacrificed too much for his son and now wanted to reclaim some of his life with his wife. Peggy was upset whenever she perceived Jim's anger and impatience seeping out, as she thought that Jake was very sensitive and would be hurt by such feelings. She also wished that Jim would take some joy in the more positive trajectory Jake was on and feel some shared pride in his improvement. Jim felt that his wife always put her son's wellbeing ahead of his needs. In addition, years of parental anxiety had exacted another price: They had become isolated from friends and family who did not understand Jake's challenges. They also second-guessed themselves and each other about what had caused Jake's psychiatric problems and who was to blame.

In couple therapy, we reviewed the sacrifices that they each had made in their work, with friendships, and with each other to keep searching for treatments and safe havens for Jake. They were encouraged to find satisfaction in the ways they had worked together and to be more compassionate about the impact this anxiety had had on their own relationship. In addition, I suggested that, instead of dividing up the emotional labor of caring for Jake, they try to share it. In other words, I asked them to share their anger and disappointment about not being care-free empty nesters and to share the satisfaction of seeing their son start to make small steps toward autonomy. To help them *feel less alone with caring for a son with mental illness, they joined a local chapter of National Alliance of Mental Illness, a grassroots organization that helps reduce stigma and provides education and support for families affected by mental illness.*

Clinical Questions and Interventions

Launching

Children's leave-taking is often not as simple or linear as packing them up and driving them to college when they are 18-year-olds. Many young adults take longer to leave home, or return home for periods even after they have launched. For couples, this is a time of transition too, and can be fraught with expectations about how it is supposed to go. It is often a fulcrum around which couples reflect on their parenting years behind them and look ahead to the uncertainty of being alone together again.

- "What happened to your parents' relationship when you left home? How were you affected by decisions that your parents made about their relationship, work, and retirement? Do you hope to repeat or do differently some of their experiences of late middle age?"
- "What are your expectations about how children become independent? Is it when they go to college, pay for their own apartment and health insurance, marry, have children, make their own decisions about work? In what ways are your ideas about launching informed by your family of origin, race, or ethnicity, or by your own experiences of leaving home?"
- "Do you have differences of opinion about launching that are familiar or surprising?"
- "Do you reflect together on the job you have done so far as parents?"

Readjusting to Marriage as Primary Relationship

Once spouses traverse to becoming empty-nest couples, there is a rise in marital satisfaction, particularly if the children are perceived to be doing well on their own (Bouchard, 2017; Dennerstein et al., 2002; Gorchoff et al., 2008). The most difficult issue is usually not missing the children, but adjusting to the marriage as the primary relationship (Bouchard & McNair, 2016). In one study of both same- and different-sex couples who had been together for an average of 30 years, two factors predicted satisfaction, regardless of sexual orientation—containment of relational conflict and the capacity to share innermost feelings and thoughts with one's partner (MacKey, Diemer, & O'Brien, 2004). Even when one partner was avoidant of conflict, if he or she could explain his or her avoidance, usually tracing it to family-of-origin patterns, the relationship was protected. Other couples who had difficulty expressing differences recognized that compensatory qualities like kindness, loyalty, equitable division of labor offset the lack of expressiveness.

- "What are the areas of conflict for you? Is the content different than it was when your children were home? Have you discovered any ways to contain conflict so that it does not take up as much time and energy?"
- "What are aspects of each other that you are finding out about one another now that you can focus without the distractions of full-time parenting?"
- "What are some of the qualities that you have come to treasure in your partner?"
- "Are there new creative activities, political pursuits, adventures, books to read aloud, spiritual journeys that you hope to engage in with one another?"

Sexual Intimacy

As older couples age, lack of lubrication for women and erectile difficulties for men may make vaginal sex challenging. As one man in his mid-60s reflected, "Sex is more like a roller coaster than a rocket ship. If my wife is okay with erections that come and go and come again, we do fine." Many couples will stop all activity when men are unable to maintain erections sufficient for vaginal penetration (Waite et al., 2009). It is important for clinicians to ask about sexual functioning in a way that does not focus just on intercourse.

- "What are some things you do just for fun? I am not asking just about sex, but anything you do for pleasure. Do you do those together? Only after you have finished your work or tasks for the day? How do you feel about these activities?"
- "Tell me about your sexual intimacy with one another. Is it enjoyable, playful, satisfying, frustrating, disappointing?"
- "I would like to ask you about a range of sexual activity: Do you masturbate alone or together? Do you enjoy manual or oral stimulation of one another? Do you like to kiss? Cuddle and spoon? Do you enjoy touching or massaging one another? Do you have intercourse, vaginal or anal? Do you have orgasms? Is there other sexual activity that you enjoy?"
- "For heterosexual couples: Do you have vaginal sex? If so, to the man, are you able to keep and maintain an erection and have an orgasm? To the woman, is penetration comfortable or pleasurable? Are you lubricated enough, or do you use supplements?"
- "For gay couples: Are you each able to get and maintain an erection and have an orgasm?"
- "For lesbian couples: Is lack of desire an obstacle to sexual activity?"
- "Most people do not talk to their physicians about sexual difficulties, but it can be helpful, particularly with certain issues like erectile problems, decline in libido, and pain during intercourse."

Future Planning

This life stage has many more years behind than ahead, but that very fact makes future planning all the more poignant and charged. Couples ask: What will we do with the precious amount of time that remains? These decisions are influenced by family-of-origin experiences, gender, cultural variables, and level of satisfaction with what has come before.

- "Do you talk with each other about retirement or your next decade? How do those conversations go?"

- "Do you have similar visions about your future plans, or do they differ?"
- "At what age did your own parents retire? What did you learn about that process from their experiences?"
- "How are your thoughts about retirement influenced by finances or by your health? By involvement as caretakers to grandchildren?"
- "Are there dreams that you postponed that you want to reclaim? Do you want to move? Find a different job? Volunteer? Pursue creative activity?"
- "What are your attitudes toward continuing to work?"

In late middle age, couples must adjust to both gains and losses. Poised on the edge of old age, couples have a chance in therapy to reflect on their lives thus far, and to decide whether to stay together, make plans for retirement, build lives around caretaking, or continue in their work lives. There is often time for second chances: as caregivers, through forging different roles as grandparents than they had as parents; in their relationships, through divorce and remarriage or by revitalizing a long marriage; and with time itself, in terms of making meaningful plans for retirement. Therapists can play a critical role in helping late-middle-age couples make the most of the rapidly shifting current landscape and manage the anxiety around what is always an unpredictable future.

CHAPTER 6

Post-Retirement and Late-Life Couples

Aging, Dependency, and Role Changes

If we take a late retirement and early death, we'll just squeak by.
—B. Smaller, *New Yorker*, July 7, 2003

For age is opportunity no less
Than youth itself, though in another dress,
And as the evening twilight fades away
The sky is filled with stars invisible by day.
—Henry Wadsworth Longfellow

Due to tremendous advances in health care, the ranks of aging American adults have swelled dramatically: The population of the United States has tripled over the past century, but those over age 65 have increased 11-fold (Administration on Aging, 2010). This upward trend will continue as the proportion of adults aged 65 and older is projected to increase from 13 percent of the population in 2010 to 20 percent in 2030. The aging population has also become more racially and ethnically diverse, although health care disparities in access and treatment have taken a heavy toll on some groups. For example, life expectancy for African-American men is much lower than for White Americans. As at every stage thus far, White, heterosexual late-life marriages are studied more frequently than others. It is, for instance, difficult to estimate the number of aging LGBT couples because they have been left out of many major gerontological studies (Barranti & Cohen, 2000) and federal surveys (Institute of Medicine, 2011).

With each life stage, the variability among couples seems to grow exponentially. For late-life couples, defined as those in the period from age 65 and continuing until death, there are many different paths that couples may traverse. For starters, during this stage, a couple's health, parent, and grandparent status may vary. In addition, for some couples, this is the first many-decade-long marriage, while for others, it is a second or third marriage of shorter duration, followed by a divorce or spousal death. For some couples, one or both may be retired, or they may still be working. And, finally, the stage is composed of sub-cohorts—extended middle-age (up until 75) or old age (up to 85) or very old age (85 or older). In later life, a couple's coping strategies, based on personality traits, cultural context, and resources, become more salient in the face of losses and declining capacities. Each of these variables can shape a couple's trajectory at this stage of life.

Despite all of this variability, several themes and issues predominate in the research on aging couples. Many couples in late life will make the decision to retire, and then face subsequent choices about how to spend their time in ways that offer meaning, structure, and companionship. Retirement is one of the most relationship-altering events in a couple's life. As work ties are severed, time spent with one's spouse will likely increase, making the marital relationship central. In one study, couples in their 80s spent 50 percent of their waking hours with their spouses (Waldinger, 2010). Couples who have been very focused on their careers and on parenting will be especially challenged by the shift to being home alone together. As Dorothy Parker wryly remarked about a husband's retirement from a wife's perspective: "I married him for better or for worse, but not for lunch." Some couples, of course, will delight in finally having plenty of time to spend together, without having to juggle commitments to work, children, and parents. Other couples will defer retirement until they become grandparents, substituting one way to be productive and needed with another. Couples who have not had children evince no difference in wellbeing compared with their counterparts who are parents and grandparents (Zhang & Hayward, 2001). If late-life contentment is not defined by parent status, intensity of engagement in voluntary and charitable work seems to be. In one study, older childfree couples were found to be more actively engaged in voluntary and charitable work than a similarly aged cohort with children (Albertini & Kohli, 2009).

Increased Physical Vulnerabilities and Illnesses

Late life is often marked by chronic illness or disabilities in one or both partners. For example, Alzheimer's is reported to occur between five and 13 percent in those over age 65, and increases to 43 percent in those age 85 and older (Alzheimer's Association, 2011). Hearing loss affects 30 percent of adults between ages 65 and 74, and 50 percent between ages 75 and 79 (Gomez & Madey, 2011). With physical frailty and illness comes more emphasis on caregiving and care-receiving in a marriage. A supportive, warm relationship offers important safeguards against the depleting strain of being a caretaker (Bookwala, 2012) and is an important resource as couples turn to one another to make difficult end-of-life decisions (Carr, Boerner, & Moorman, 2013).

There are many studies linking social relationships in late life to health and extended mortality. Aging well turns out to be not just about access to excellent health care; it is also about being in a positive, nurturing relationship. In a landmark study, researchers found that a lack of social relationships was as much a risk factor for poor health among the elderly as was cigarette smoking, high blood pressure, and obesity (House, Landis, & Umberson, 1988). A later meta-analysis of 148 prospective studies examining links between social connection and longevity found a 50 percent increased likelihood of survival among individuals who enjoyed strong social ties (Holt-Lunstad, Smith, & Layton, 2010).

Not surprisingly, these health benefits are derived only from positive relationships, as individuals in poor marriages exhibit worse health than those who are divorced (Williams, 2003). The stress of lonely or high-conflict marriages may actually accelerate the aging of the immune system. Chronic stress, which is typical of ongoing marital conflict, produces increases in circulating stress hormones, such as cortisol, epinephrine, and norepinephrine, contributing to elevated heart rate and blood pressure. In older people with chronic medical conditions, these effects of negative marital experiences may accelerate physical decline. Stress takes a cumulative toll such that poor marital quality is especially damaging to the health of late-life couples (Umberson et al., 2006). Couples who perceive their relationship as negative and stressful are more at risk for obesity (Birditt et al., 2016) and high blood pressure (Burditt et al., 2015).

Positive marital satisfaction in late life also cushions the impact of health problems on mood. Waldinger (2010) recorded daily pain and mood reports of 47 octogenarian couples, married for an average of 41 years, and found an inverse relationship between poorer health and happiness among maritally dissatisfied couples, but not for couples in satisfying relationships. Those in less happy marriages seemed more vulnerable to the daily impact of health problems on their mood. Or, put another way, marital satisfaction seems to protect couples from the full impact of physical ups and downs on mood.

While stress harms both men and women, women's health and wellbeing are particularly vulnerable to marital conflict. Unhappily married women have more physical and mental health problems than happily married women. For example, in a sample of 292 women with a history of coronary heart disease, Orth-Gomeret et al. (2000) found that marital stress almost tripled the risk of recurrent coronary events over a five-year period. In a review of 45 articles that looked at the data on both spouses in couples 65 and older, researchers found many gender imbalances (Walker & Luszcz, 2009). When a husband was depressed, dissatisfied, or suffering from an illness, his feelings had significant negative effects on his wife: Both he and his wife complained of more depression and life stress. When a woman reported marital or health distress, however, only she experienced more depressive symptoms and life stress (Whiffen & Gottlieb, 1989). This asymmetry can be explained perhaps by the notion that a man who views his marriage unfavorably may still derive benefits of caretaking and practical support from his wife (Carr et al., 2014), while a woman who is unhappily married does not reap these same advantages.

Disabilities and diminishment of good health are not the only losses that older couples face. By the time couples reach their 70s and 80s, most have lost friends, siblings, and colleagues. Additionally, thoughts of one's own and one's partner's mortality are more present. There can be a serious taking stock of one's life with the shortening time horizon ahead, as well as a wish to think about legacy and to address end-of-life issues.

Positive Trends in Late-Life Couples

Yet, despite the sobering aspects that commonly accompany aging, older couples are generally happier, spend less time managing conflict with one another, and have more relaxed, flexible gender roles than do younger couples. Several researchers have noted a curvilinear model of relationships over time: Early marriage is marked by strong feelings of connectedness and a high degree of conflict, while in the middle years of child-rearing, positive feelings are lower and conflict increases. In general, older couples' relationships are characterized by close companionship, mutual support, and very little conflict (Condie, 1989; Levenson, Carstensen, & Gottman, 1994; Carstensen, Isaacowitz, & Charles, 1999; Yang, 2008).

The reduction of conflict in older couples has been explained as a function of aging: With limited time ahead, couples choose to spend less time relitigating the same fights they have fought for decades. In a laboratory setting, when elderly couples were asked to re-enact a fight, researchers had difficulty motivating these couples to comply, as they seemed almost bored by the instruction.[1] When elderly couples do fight, they are more likely than their middle-aged counterparts to interject expressions of affection, to have better emotion regulation, and to engage with less anger, disgust, and belligerence (Carstensen, Gottman, & Levenson, 1995).

The impact of aging is experienced in other realms besides conflict. Older couples tend to be more focused on the present than the past. They pay more attention to emotions and value a smaller number of deeper connections. Older couples may be more likely to accept the relationship as it is, rather than to be looking ahead to a time when the marriage can be transformed. Instead, they tend to focus more on what it is good and may try to ignore the negative aspects of their relationship (Carstensen, Isaacowitz, & Charles, 1999).

More Mutuality in Gender Roles and Dependency Needs

The observation that late-life couples exhibit more gender-role equity than their younger counterparts has been attributed to the end of daily parenting and the shrinking of time spent with friends and work colleagues: One result is that couples focus jointly on the importance of

---

[1] Dr. Bob Waldinger, personal communication, Boston, MA, October 6, 2017.

their relationship (Carr et al., 2014). For spouses who followed a tra-ditional homemaker or breadwinner template, the husband's retirement may usher in the reduction of power disparities, as they now are mutually dependent on another for companionship and stimulation. Perhaps even more significantly, physical frailties and a shrinking of social and work contacts make it obvious that mutual dependency is an advantage, rather than a weakness. Many partnered men and women realize that their rela-tionship is essential and precious, and that mutual support in the face of other losses is critical. This reckoning with the changes wrought by aging seems to usher in greater gender equity (Carr et al., 2014).

One of the greatest challenges for late-life relationships is the salience of dependency needs in the face of frailty, illness, and fears about mor-tality. Spouses will need to depend on one another and be willing to be depended on. The template and patterns for dependency were often cre-ated during their childhood, when they learned whether their parents could be counted on to respond to their needs for comfort, closeness, and care. Researchers have found that octogenarian couples who had expe-rienced warm, nurturing family environments as children, were better equipped to accept the vulnerabilities associated with aging. Most strik-ing, these couples who had experienced secure attachments as children were able to embrace the two sides of late-life dependency—depending on their spouse for care and comfort, and in turn, offering that safety and connection to their partner. Along the way, those same securely attached couples also reported greater marital satisfaction, better mood, and less conflict than their less-secure counterparts (Waldinger & Schulz, 2016; Waldinger et al., 2015).

As in the Previous Stage, Sexual Intimacy Is Still Important

Our knowledge of sexual functioning and health in late-life couples is quite scant, as researchers have largely overlooked this topic when study-ing aging. For example, there is no mention of sexuality research in *Living Long and Well in the 21st Century: Strategic Directions for Research on Aging*, a policy document from the National Institute of Aging (2007). When considering older couples' sexuality, the focus needs to go beyond inquiries about frequency of intercourse and orgasm to include questions about sexual contact of any kind, particularly solo and partnered masturbation, and oral sex. When asking about sexual functioning, therapists should also ask about the couple's own perceived satisfaction with their sexual life, rather than imposing an *objective* standard (Delamater, 2012).

Many late-life couples continue to engage in sexual activity and to regard it as important. Among those 65 to 74 years old, more than half of those individuals had rates of sexual activity that were not dissimilar from those reported in a study of younger sexually active adults, ages 18 to 59 years of age (Laumann et al., 1994). In an older cohort, those 75 to 85 years old, 54 percent reported engaging in sexual activity at least two to three times a month, and 23 percent had some form of sex once a week or more (Lindau et al., 2007). In general, among those who remain sexual active, rates of sexual engagement remain fairly consistent through age 75, and for some couples, well beyond.

Sexual desire may be the most affected aspect of sexual functioning in aging couples. In one study, reports of feeling sexual desire a few times a week declined from 76 percent in men aged 45 to 59 years to 43 percent among men aged 60 to 74 years, and to only 17 percent in men over 75 years old. Among women, the comparable percentages were 36, 11, and 4 percent, respectively, although the rates were higher in a similar age group of Black and Latina women (Delamater & Koepsel, 2015). But a lack of sexual desire is not dispositive when it comes to sexual activity: Couples may still seek sexual engagement with one another, absent of libido, knowing that once they begin touching or kissing one another, they will feel pleasure and connection.

Late-life couples do not treat cessation of sexual activity casually, as a foregone conclusion of aging. Instead, both men and women in a study of late-life sexuality reported that they were bothered by a partner's lack of sexual responsiveness. For women, having an emotionally responsive partner can compensate for his not being sexually responsive, whereas for men, having close friendships can moderate their distress regarding sexual difficulties (Hirayama & Walker, 2011). In other words, when disappointed about their sexual relationship, women find comfort within the relationship, and men do so from male friendships. The takeaway here is that while many elderly couples remain sexually active, those who have given up sexual engagement feel the lack and try to compensate for this loss.

Common Presentations

Secrets That Emerge in Late Life

The quickening approach of mortality in late life may bring urgency to secrets that have been kept for decades. Spouses may disagree about whether to divulge tightly held information to their children and grand-children about birth stories, trauma, substance abuse, sexual orientation, and money. One man in his 70s, after recovering medically from a sui-cide attempt, divulged a secret he had been keeping for years from his wife and children: He was bankrupt and had hoped that his life insur-ance would provide for his family. A retired surgeon who had kept his substance-abuse history a secret from his children, decided to share it when his granddaughter was arrested for driving under the influence. No longer fearful that he might lose his medical license, and urged by his wife who had wanted him to share this history with their own children, he hoped that sharing the secret now would not only help the next gener-ation, but would also repair a long-standing disagreement with his wife. In another couple, a husband and wife, both survivors of the Holocaust, waited until they were in their 80s to share details of their time in a concentration camp in Poland. They did not want this important part of their family history to be lost when they died, but they had not wanted to burden their children with the traumatic details of their earlier lives.

Profound Disappointment About Dependency and Intimacy

If mutual dependency is a major hallmark of this stage, it is also a task that can be their Waterloo.

Helen (70) and Mitch (78), a Euro-American couple, faced a crisis in their 30-year marriage when Mitch felt vulnerable after a heart attack and was profoundly disappointed by his perception that his wife had not been available when he really needed her. This was a second marriage for both, with no children from this marriage or from their previous ones. When they first came to therapy, they were both recently retired—Helen from her job as a hospital administrator, and Mitch from his job as a CEO at a pharmaceutical company. They both complained of feeling distant from one another and lonely in the marriage, despite now spending most of their time with each other. Helen pointed to Mitch's heart attack and bypass surgery a year earlier as the point at which they had started to drift apart. Mitch agreed that his illness had been a crossroads in their marriage. When asked to elaborate, he said that his heart issues were the first time he could remember ever needing his wife. He was terrified he was going to die, terrified of the procedures he endured, and had felt abandoned by Helen during his hospital stay. He remembered that, "She always seemed too busy and preoccupied to really spend time with me." Helen, though initially defensive, eventually admitted that she was frightened by Mitch's vulnerability, as he had always been such a self-reliant and confident man, and she had not known how to comfort him when he was sick. She wanted to make it up to him now and suggested they work on their sexual relationship as a way to get closer. Helen hoped that this offer to rekindle their sexual relationship would help repair her sexual withdrawal from Mitch years ago, when he had tried repeatedly to engage her sexually.

In therapy, they decided to focus on their sexual relationship, and I suggested several sex therapy exercises for them to try at home. But, after weeks of Helen telling me she had initiated the homework without any response from Mitch, I asked if there was something else getting in his way. After a long pause, Mitch revealed that he had been going to a masseuse for sex since his heart attack, and in the last few months had fallen in love with her. He described this woman, half his age, as caring, loving, and thoughtful toward him. Helen responded in a way that surprised Mitch. "Go ahead and pursue the relationship. I can't believe that she really loves you. She's just taking advantage of an old, wealthy man. I'll wait for you and be here after you figure it out." With that, the couple left my office and I never saw them again. Ten years later, I stumbled upon Mitch's obituary and discovered that he had married the masseuse.

I cannot be sure what prompted Mitch and Helen to end their marriage. It seems likely that there was an irrevocable rupture that occurred when Mitch's illness altered the power dynamics of the couple. He stopped being the self-reliant, competent, autonomous husband and revealed, instead, his need for nurture and caretaking. When Helen withdrew out of fear and discomfort, he appears not to have forgiven her. In the relationship with the younger woman, he found someone who seemed at ease with his dependency needs. Before the heart attack, Mitch had not experienced himself as needing to lean on his wife, but a life-threatening illness brought these dependency needs to the fore, and exposed a relational element that had been optional at early stages but was essential in old age.

Conflicts and Estrangements in the Younger Generation

Just because the children are grown up and living independently, often with families of their own, does not mean that late-life couples stop worrying about their offspring. Compounding the complexity of the elders' worry is the added dimension that their own children are often providing care to them. In this mix of caretaking up and down the generational tree, relationships both between generations and within the same middle generation of siblings can become strained and conflicted.

David (75) and Ruth (74) are a Jewish couple, married for almost 50 years with two daughters, Rebecca (43) and Leah (41). When the parents came for couple therapy, David had just retired from being an English professor at a college hundreds of miles away, where he had lived four days a week and commuted home to Boston on the weekends. He and Ruth were now living together full-time for the first time in decades. Unlike many late-life couples, David and Ruth were dismayed at the tension and flare-up of conflicts that were more intense now than at any previous time in their relationship. David felt untethered and lost, and he sought out constant companionship from Ruth. Trying to finish writing a memoir about her family's escape from Nazi Germany, Ruth rebuffed her husband's invitations to travel, go to cultural events, and have friends over, disclosing that she was terrified that she would die before her book was completed. She wanted time alone to concentrate on her writing. David fought with Ruth about her being unavailable, while Ruth retaliated with charges of his selfishness and lack of respect for her work.

Adding to their marital conflict was tension over their daughters' recent estrangement from one another. Rebecca, 43, after years of infertility treatment, had two adopted sons, and Leah, 40, after recovering from an opioid addiction, had recently given birth to a son. Each daughter felt that her parents had paid more attention to the other daughter during that sister's medical crisis of infertility or addiction. This resentment now expressed itself by the daughters not wanting to attend family gatherings together. David was

*enraged at his daughters' behavior and wanted to "read them the riot act,"
while Ruth insisted that David's expression of outrage would only make things
worse. For her part, Ruth did not know what to do and was feeling distraught
that the family could not spend time all together.*

*When their daughters were growing up, David and Ruth described their
family of four as close, warm, and supportive. This family stood in contrast
to each of their own childhoods, which had both been characterized by early
maternal deaths. As their therapist, I wondered whether the current rupture
of family cohesion was particularly painful, insofar as it resonated with their
childhood experiences of fragmentation and loss. Creating a tight-knit family
had been reparative, and now their daughters' rift with one another threatened to destroy what they had built.*

*In our work, I suggested that they step back from their efforts to corral
their daughters into forced family events. Instead, focusing on shoring up relationships with each daughter separately might go a long way to repairing each
daughter's grievances. Also important was that David and Ruth refrain from
discussing one sister with the other, a destructive pattern that had developed
from their hurt and frustration. In addition, I encouraged them to continue to
invite their daughters to family events, making it clear to each daughter when
her sister was invited too, and then leaving it up to their daughters to figure
out what they wanted to do. I wondered whether the daughters were also trying to distract their parents from their own marital squabbles by offering them
a sibling fight to focus on. Perhaps, their daughters would be relieved to learn
that their parents had sought help from a couple therapist.*

*Over time, David and Ruth understood their fights and eventually
arrived at a new equilibrium with one another; they also told their daughters
they were getting help for their marriage. They reminded each other not to
talk with one daughter about the other. They invited each daughter and her
family over for meals, and joined them at playgrounds and parks, and they
made sure to be available to babysit for all their grandsons. Perhaps, these
changes paved the way for the impact of an unplanned, unscripted event.
Rebecca's five-year-old son begged for his aunt to be invited to his birthday
party, and then again to Thanksgiving. Leah did not want to say "no" to her
nephew, and so she agreed to come with her family to both family events. They
were tense but not unpleasant, and soon family gatherings resumed without
much fanfare.*

Sometimes, being a couple therapist feels like being a gardener, tending a couple relationship that is a small plot of land. Together we plant some new seeds and hope that new behaviors and ways of communication may take root and sprout. Occasionally, there is a *volunteer* flower that just shows up, like the grandson's innocent insistence that his aunt attend his birthday celebration.

Clinical Questions and Interventions

Day-to-Day Life of Spending Time Together

Given that most late-life couples will be spending more time with one another than they had at previous stages, it is important to ask specifically about day-to-day interactions. Moreover, as physical vulnerabilities increase, they may have an impact on a couple's mobility and activity level. So, you might ask:

- "How much time do you spend with each other during a typical day?"
- "What activities, friendships, hobbies, do you each do on your own? Is there any change you would want to make in the balance of time spent with your partner and time spent alone or with other people?"
- "If you have any health issues, how do they affect your day-to-day life with one another?"
- "Are there work, travel, volunteer, or creative pursuits that you would like to make time for?"
- "Are you happy with your living situation? Do you talk about moving to a smaller place, or in with family, or to a retirement community? If you have already moved, how have you adjusted to a new living situation?"

Sexual Intimacy

As sexual engagement continues to be important for most couples well into late life, it is important that clinicians always inquire about this aspect of a relationship. Questions must be inclusive of sexual encounters that extend beyond vaginal and anal penetration, and may not involve orgasm, as these are the elements of sex that may fluctuate with disabilities and diminished health. Some key questions:

- "You have not mentioned your sexual relationship. Is that an important part of your life with one another? Would you like to talk about that with me?"
- "If you have a health problem or are taking medications that might affect your sexual functioning, have you discussed any sexual issues with your physician?"
- "Have you made accommodations in your sexual relationship due to health or other issues? Do you talk with each other about any changes in your sexual life?"
- "Many older couples discover that they enjoy different ways of giving and receiving pleasure than they did when they were younger. For example, oral sex and manual stimulation, massage, and the use of fantasy, sometimes become more important than intercourse. How does this go for the two of you?"
- "Are there ways that you enjoy being sexually intimate with one another now that are different, even better, than what you experienced at earlier stages of your lives?"

Dependency and Closeness

One of the biggest challenges of aging is the ability and willingness to depend on one's spouse for solace, comfort, and companionship, and to be willing to be depended upon by one's spouse. These questions may be helpful:

- "Whom do you confide in? Whom can you talk to about things that are most important to you?"
- "If you have needed help during an illness or after a surgery, have you been able to turn to your partner?"
- "If your health were to deteriorate, would you trust your spouse to care for you?"

Relationships with Other Family Members and Friends

A common feature of aging is that most individuals find that their social worlds constrict as they focus on a smaller number of meaningful relationships, often with family members and a few close friends.

- "What are your relationships like with your children, grandchildren, in-laws, and siblings? Are any of these relationships more conflicted or more distant than you wish?"
- "Do you get together with friends you have known well?"
- "Do you have a community or a group of friends that you and your spouse enjoy, depend on, and spend time with?"
- "Are you a member of an organization that you really care about such as a church, nonprofit, book club, meditation center?"

As the numbers of late-life couples increase, more couple therapists will be required to be knowledgeable about the many challenges and gratifications of this life phase. On the one hand, older couples commonly enjoy a lower level of conflict and a higher degree of connectedness than couples at early life stages. This positive development is attributable largely to shifts in couples' time perspectives: The quantity of time spent together increases when couples' social worlds constrict after retirement and losses of friends. Aging often sharpens the focus on the present, a focus that leads couples to be more accepting of each other's shortcomings and past transgressions.

On the other hand, aging often brings an increase in illness and disability, as well as recognition of the unstoppable approach of impending mortality. These inevitable dimensions of aging mean that late-life couples may come to rely almost exclusively on one another for comfort, companionship, and practical assistance. Working with older couples to improve their relationships allows for a double impact: Therapists can help improve intimacy and connection when a couple's relationship is often at the center of their life; additionally, elders' physical health gets a boost and a buffer when marital interactions are positive and satisfying. Perhaps the most challenging event of late life is the subject of the next chapter—facing end-of-life issues with one's partner, saying goodbye, and, for the widowed member of the couple, carrying on alone.

CHAPTER 7

Illness and Death

Bereavement is not the truncation of married love but one of its regular phases—like the honeymoon. What we want is to live our marriage well and faithfully through that phase too.
                                               —C.S. Lewis, *A Grief Observed*

People want to share memories, pass on wisdoms and keepsakes, settle relationships, establish their legacies, make peace with God, and ensure that those left behind will be okay. They want to end their stories on their own terms.
                                               —Atul Gawande, *Being Mortal*

Every couple relationship will end eventually, either through death, divorce, or separation. It is also true that relationships will live on in memory, in offspring, and in stories. Since end-of-life issues are the most profound challenges that couples face, the focus here will be on death as an ending, with attention paid to working with couples where one partner is experiencing a serious, life-threatening illness. The challenges of working with couples who are divorcing are beyond the scope of this book, but the reader can find guidance from several helpful resources (Heatherington & Kelly, 2002; Lyness, 2012; Ahrons, 2016).

Clinical Issues During Illness

Much has been written about the salutary effects of a good marriage on the physical health of a couple. Positive spousal support has been found to lessen the experience of pain (Coan, Schaefer, & Davis, 2006) and the need for pain medications, and also to improve recovery after surgery (King et al., 1993), and to lower the risk of mortality (Roble et al., 2014). Researchers have found that positive marital quality is an even greater predictor of longevity than any biological marker in patients with conges-tive heart failure (Coyne et al., 2001). But no marriage, however robust and supportive, can stave off serious illness indefinitely. And, some cou-ples bypass serious illness altogether, by dying as a result of an accident, by suicide, or by dying suddenly without any previously identified disease.

When couples do confront serious illness, it is sensible for a cou-ple therapist to reverse the relationship of marriage and illness: That is, instead of wondering how the marriage can help stave off illness, it is time for the therapists to ask how is their relationship transformed by serious illness and what will be helpful to them as they confront a chronic illness or the last stage of the life cycle?

In general, serious illness magnifies the overall quality of any relation-ship. For many couples, it will bring them together in a state of greater intimacy and connection than any time before. They will experience a laser-like focus on what is meaningful to them about their relationship, with concomitant feelings of gratitude and love for each other, even while they also deal with the very real stresses of navigating a complex health system and coping with the uncertainties of illness. Confrontation with the finitude of time, regardless of the age of the couple, usually shifts a couple's perspective from future-oriented goals to valuing their most inti-mate relationships (Fung & Carstensen, 2006). For some couples, how-ever, this sharpening of focus may not lead to enhanced connection, but to the desire to separate.

Following the life-threatening complications after Arthur's (66) bypass surgery, he felt deeply disappointed and hurt by how distant and cold he experienced Betty (62) during his hospital stay. While Betty felt badly that she had let Arthur down during his illness, she also realized that, after a child-hood looking after her siblings and a professional life devoted to caretaking, she recoiled at assuming that role in her marriage. Acknowledging that she was not honoring her wedding vow of "in sickness and health," she made the difficult decision to leave the marriage. She realized that she did not want to promise that she could handle Arthur's medical vulnerabilities differently going forward.

John Rolland, a physician and family therapist working with families facing medical illness, had the keen insight decades ago that clinicians need more than a classification system that clusters illnesses purely around their biological criteria. Instead, he proposed a typology that looks at four different ways that a couple's relationship interweaves with disease (Rolland, 1987). First are the *characteristics of the illness itself.* If, for example, the onset of the illness was sudden, as with a stroke or spinal cord injury, the couple will have to tolerate a surplus of emotion, a sudden shift in roles, and a great deal of involvement from previously unknown outside helpers and resources. By contrast, if the illness has a more gradual onset, as with Parkinson's, the couple may have more time to adapt but also more uncertainty to cope with.

Another aspect of the fingerprint of the illness is its pace of unfolding; whether it is progressive, as with amyotrophic lateral sclerosis (ALS), requiring a couple to keep adjusting to increasing deterioration and severity of symptoms; or constant, as after a stroke, where the couple lives with a stable change; or relapsing or episodic, as with multiple sclerosis, where a couple has the added stress of oscillating between periods of stability and crisis with uncertainty about when a person's health status may switch.

The types of physical or mental limitations that accompany the illness also have different effects on a relationship. Furthermore, one member of the couple may feel that the loss of mobility, for example, is devastating, while the other member regards the same limitation as less life-altering. The gradual loss of memory and other cognitive functioning associated with dementia will often take the greatest toll on a couple's ability to connect with one another, although many couples manage to hold on to enduring parts of their partner, like traits of kindness and humor, even as so much other cognitive functioning fades away.

Illnesses have different impacts on a relationship depending on the prognosis: If it is certain and imminent, the couple may have little time for end-of-life conversations, attention to wills and funeral plans; but more often, the prognosis is less certain, so that the couple does not know whether to pivot to the end, or live with constant vigilance and suspended plans. Some couples will continue doing all that they can, not changing course or holding back on plans, until the illness stops them.

The *life-cycle of the illness* is the second dimension highlighted by Rolland.

The crisis period when a couple is struggling to make sense of symptoms through medical tests, appointments with doctors, and finding a diagnosis is a time of great stress. Couples have to find and establish a relationship with strangers who will become the health care team, often cope with pain, and try to support each other during a time of uncertainty. Dr. Leah Rosenberg, a palliative care and hospice physician at Massachusetts General Hospital, notes that this is a crucial time to process with the couple because their spoken and unspoken plan for their future has been disrupted.[1] From the initial diagnosis until the issues of end of life, the couple then faces the everyday stressors of living with chronic illness. The main task here is for both partners to feel that their needs for comfort and dependency are attended to, while some autonomy is allowed for each. During the terminal phase, the inevitability of death is in the forefront as the couple faces separation, grief, life review, and legacy.

The third dimension of Rolland's typology is the *couple's developmental stage*. Serious illness, while always disruptive and unwelcome, is particularly difficult when it is also untimely. A growing number of parents with young children are diagnosed with life-threatening illnesses. The increase may be due to earlier and better detection of illnesses and to parents starting families at a later age, when some illnesses, like diabetes or heart disease, are more common. The National Cancer Institute estimates that at least 18 percent of the cancer patients diagnosed in the past years, and 14 percent of all cancer survivors are parenting a child under the age of 18 (Weaver et al., 2010). When a parent has a serious illness, the couple must figure out how much information to share with their children in a way that is developmentally appropriate, as well as how to maintain routines and stability for children in the midst of uncertainty and disruptions from medical appointments, pain, and the capacity to perform customary parenting roles and tasks (Moore & Rauch, 2015; Moore & Rauch, 2017). Parenting At a Challenging Time (PACT) is a unique parent guidance program, initiated in 1997 by a child psychiatrist, Dr. Paula Rauch, at Massachusetts General Hospital, that offers consultations to parents with many different medical conditions. PACT clinicians have helped thousands of parents figure out how best to cope with illness while continuing

---

[1] Dr. Leah Rosenberg, personal communication, November 16, 2017.

to support their children's development and growth (Moore & Rauch, 2017; Rauch & Muriel, 2006; http://mghpact.org/).[2]

In an interview, Dr. Rauch[3] reflected on some of the special burdens shouldered by younger couples when one partner faces a life-threatening illness: "For younger couples who are facing end-of-life challenges while their peer group is stressing about buying a house, dealing with intrusive in-laws, (and other issues at mid-life), it can feel like being catapulted into another universe." The couple and their friends may not yet have mourned the loss of their own parents, so that death is a process that is uncharted territory, and may make the couple feel particularly isolated. While death at late life is also painful, there are "peers who have walked the same path, and that helps ground the couple, especially the well partner" (Rauch, 2017, interview). There has likely been some rehearsal and anticipation when a serious illness occurs after a long life together.

In addition to timing, marital status may also complicate the couple's experience of grief and end of life. While financial and health care directives can be taken care of outside of marriage, widowhood in the context of marriage confers particular social recognition. In one study of older LGBTQ individuals, Lannutti (2010) found that, as spouses anticipated death, they were reassured to think that their widowed partners would be given the support and emotional recognition that accompanies marriage. Among elderly LGBT couples, who came of age during more homophobic times, and who have hidden their sexual orientation from family, friends, and co-workers, the death of a partner may go unacknowledged. It is important to ask bereaved LGBT individuals whom they can count on to talk about their loss and to grieve with them.

The fourth dimension in Roland's typology contextualizes illness within the *intergenerational history* of a family, including their cultural

---

[2] As my colleagues at MGH include the founder (Dr. Paula Rauch) and the Associate Director (Dr. Cynthia Moore) of PACT, a nationally renowned, first-of its-kind service, I have taken advantage of this resource and included interviews in this chapter. In addition, as I have less clinical experience working with end-of-life couples than with couples at other stages, I am most appreciative to have access to clinicians with decades of engagement with this population.

[3] Dr. Paula Rauch, personal communication, October 10, 2017.

attitudes toward pain, doctors, and serious medical problems. Complaining about pain, for example, is regarded differently depending on the cultural context. One Irish-American husband admired his wife's upbeat attitude during a grueling round of chemotherapy, "She was so stoic, brave, and never complained." By contrast, a Jewish-American woman recalled with gratitude that during her husband's last weeks before dying, "I was so glad that he let us know when he was in pain, so we could give him enough morphine." Dr. Rosenberg recalls the evangelical language and talk about miracles she used when in palliative care training in the South, as compared to the more stiff-upper-lip, skeptical, and cognitive language that she often adopts at a Northeast teaching hospital.

In addition to a couple's cultural attitudes, sometimes shared and sometimes different from one another, are their childhood experiences witnessing illness and death in their respective families. A person who observed the painful death of a family member may be more comfortable considering hospice care as soon as it is recommended. A spouse who watched a parent suffer a rapid demise from diagnosis to death may be less familiar with how to live with the uncertainties of a chronic illness.

Conversations About Illness and End of Life

Often, when a spouse is seriously ill, the couple therapy has a pace that tracks the rhythm of medical appointments. A couple therapist might relax a weekly therapy frame and meet with a couple when they come to a hospital for medical treatment, talk on the phone, or make a home visit if one member is too frail to leave home. Reframing an illness as a problem that is happening to both members of the couple, even though it is inside the body of only one partner, can be helpful in maintaining a relational stance. When an illness is seen as a shared problem, the couple can collaborate on facing it together.

Previous Experiences That Inform the Couple Now

Couples bring their own histories with illness and dying from their cultural backgrounds and their families of origin. Additionally, a couple has likely navigated other crises, perhaps medical ones, but also troubles with children, job losses, or marital challenges. A therapist can inquire about these previous emotional trials with an eye on discovering the couple's strengths and coping strategies in the face of adversity. Some questions to ask:

- "What other difficult situations have you navigated? What did you learn about each other's coping strategies that might be helpful to you now?"
- "In each of your families, whom do you talk to about serious matters?"
- "What experiences have you had in your families growing up dealing with serious medical illness? How did your parents talk about pain, health care providers, caretaking, illness, death? And, what did you observe that maybe was not talked about?"
- "Was there secrecy shrouding a family member's illness?"
- "Were there negative experiences or positive ones dealing with hospitals and medical teams?"

Inviting the Illness Narrative

Often, couples have not had the opportunity to fully tell their shared story of medical illness to anyone. The medical parts have been shared with health care providers, and the emotional aspects told to friends and family, but likely with some restraint. Asking a couple to describe the illness' onset, diagnostic process and treatment, as well as their understanding of and their feelings about the illness, can be very helpful (McDaniel, Hepworth, & Doherty, 2009). An invitation to talk about the illness narrative may go like this:

> "I'd like to know more about how this illness has been for the two of you. You've both been through a lot. I imagine that some of your experiences dealing with this sickness have been similar, and some have been different. Tell me about it, from the beginning."

A couple therapist may listen for similarities and differences in the couple's understanding and experience of the illness. In a marriage, each member may have different attitudes toward the medical team, a different understanding of the prognosis or of the cause of the illness, and different degrees of willingness to talk about the illness. Often, each member of the couple will divvy up the emotional tasks around coping with illness, so that one is more the voice for courage and perseverance, while the other speaks about fear and worry; one feels despair and the other hope; one seeks out information from the internet and providers, while the other eschews more input. A therapist might point out that it is common for couples to share these difficult emotional tasks by dividing them up, and it may be helpful for them to talk with each other about their different emotional perspectives.

In the face of painful emotion, it is human nature to project what is unbearable onto a partner. A husband may insist, for example, that he is fine but is worried about his partner. It is quite common for an ill partner to defer his or her own wishes to stop aggressive treatment and continue to pursue therapies holding the belief that this is the partner's wish (Gawande, 2016). Members of a couple, particularly ones who have been together for many years, may not even be certain as to what each one wants, or what is being expressed on behalf of the other.

Issues of Loss

Loss is at the heart of serious illness. There is the loss of good health and a body that is dependable; the loss of the capacity to work; the loss of a sexual relationship; and the loss of the ability to perform daily activities like going to the bathroom, driving a car, and getting dressed. Many of these losses lead to role disruptions, requiring one person to take over household tasks performed for years by the other spouse. The losses also lead to asymmetry, where one partner becomes the caretaker and the other the one needing care. This may be particularly difficult when the expectation was in the opposite direction. For example, a significantly younger wife expected that she would be the eventual caretaker of her much older husband, but when she was diagnosed with stage-four ovarian cancer, their unspoken deal was upended. The role disruption may also be especially difficult when there have been clearly delineated gender roles. It can be particularly frightening for a man who has valued autonomy and dependability to accept caregiving and to relinquish being able to drive, handle finances, and take care of his own bodily functions.

Resist the Pull of Illness to Dominate All Aspects of the Relationship

While a life-threatening illness will draw much of a couple's energy and affect, it is important to help them talk about topics other than the illness and have identities separate from being a couple facing illness. It may be useful to externalize the illness by observing, for example, that "the cancer seems to be getting the upper hand lately, interfering with your experiencing close times together." This reframe joins the couple in relation to the illness and invites them to problem-solve about a shared dilemma. *When are you able to draw a boundary around the illness and enjoy time together, or engage in activities that you both enjoy?* Calvin Trillin, a prolific nonfiction writer, wrote in *About Alice*, a book about his deceased wife, how important it was for Alice to retain an identity separate from that of a dying person: "For Alice the measure of how you hold up in the face of a life-threatening illness was not how much you changed but how much you stayed the same, in control of your own identity" (Trillin, 2006, p. 75). This same notion can be applied to a couple's identity as well. The couple will need to oscillate between facing an illness and continuing to maintain their everyday routines and tasks, between talking about end-of life issues and focusing on what is stable and meaningful in the present.

End-of-Life Conversations

The conversations that take place from the time of terminal diagnosis to the point of death are very meaningful and important to the dying person, as well as to family members. Gawande's *Being Mortal* (2014) offers a powerful argument for having conversations about end-of-life health care so that patients choose what treatments they want and decide where and how they want to live at the end of life. These medical conversations are typically guided by a palliative care or hospice professional, but a couple therapist should be aware of the importance of recommending these discussions and, when appropriate, initiating and guiding them. Several studies have found that when patients are able to discuss their goals for end of life, they suffer less, hold on longer to the ability to engage with others, and die more peacefully. Additionally, when people are able to have substantive discussions about their end-of-life preferences, the bereaved are less likely to experience a major depression (Wright et al., 2008). In a landmark study that randomly assigned patients with stage-four lung cancer to standard oncology care or regular care plus visits with a palliative care specialist, those in the latter group had less aggressive medical intervention, experienced less suffering, and even lived 25 percent longer than those in the standard care group (Temel et al., 2010).

Here are questions from Dr. Susan Block, Professor of Psychiatry and Medicine at Harvard Medical School (Gawande, 2014), that she asks to facilitate conversation about end-of-life decisions:

- "What do you understand your prognosis to be?"
- "What are your concerns about what lies ahead?"
- "What kind of tradeoffs are you willing to make?"
- "How do you want to spend your time if your health worsens?"
- "Who do you want to make decisions if you cannot?"

In addition to conversations about end-of-life health care, there are other important topics such as focusing on saying goodbye, expressing love and gratitude, and reviewing the time spent together as a couple. In one recent study that asked 152 people to recall their final conversations with a loved one, several themes emerged: verbal and nonverbal expressions of love; advice offered about the future; the sharing of the meaning and value the relationship had provided; religious or spiritual messages; everyday talk, including reminiscing and storytelling; revisiting of relationship injuries in order to give or receive forgiveness; and review of what the couple had done well together (Keely & Generous, 2017). In another study conducted after the death of a loved one, researchers asked which end-of-life conversations the living wished they had had with their terminally ill family member (Generous & Keely, 2017). Participants indicated that they regretted not having talked about negative aspects of their relationship and about post-death arrangements, and they wished that they had asked more questions about that person's childhood experiences.

There is no perfect script that couples need to follow at the end of life, and in the face of one of the most stressful events of the life-cycle, partners deal with illness and saying goodbye the best they can. Some couples will not be able to have these conversations at all, because death comes suddenly through an accident or drug overdose. Others will simply not want to have them.

Needless to say, end-of-life conversations can be difficult and painful. Most couples have never had them before, and they may not know who should lead the discussion or choose the topics. These conversations are packed with feelings, particularly those of deep sadness, fear, anger, and uncertainty. A couple facing life-threatening illness may have different ways of expressing these feelings that can be complementary or sometimes work at cross-purposes. An ill husband may try to focus on positive thinking to protect his spouse from feeling sad about his dying, while desperately wanting to talk about the end of his life with his spouse, who is also his best friend. The well partner may not want to agitate her frail and suffering partner, or open up old wounds without knowing if there is to be sufficient time or energy to heal them. It can be very painful for a couple who has been present for each other during other life challenges to find themselves in different places, with one spouse wanting to talk about cure, and the other about dying.

Dr. Paula Rauch described a common marital dynamic she has observed in counseling couples when one partner has a life-threatening illness. From the well partner's perspective, she often hears, "I feel so bad about the person who is dying that I won't mention what is hard for me." Dr. Rauch explains, "That doesn't go well because all that bottled-up of feeling often results in intense resentment, especially in the setting of an untimely illness." More salutary for the couple is when each partner has a sense of the other one's perspective and can empathize with the other's sense of loss. The ill spouse may feel compassion for her partner who is going to be abandoned by her death, while the husband feels sorrow for what his dying partner is going to miss out on.[4] This level of deep mutual empathy in the face of serious illness, when couples are at their most raw, is a high bar.

Dr. Cynthia Moore,[5] Associate Director of the PACT program at MGH, notes that "the ill person is frequently in charge of the brakes," so

---

[4] Rauch, P. personal communication, October 10, 2017.
[5] Dr. Cynthia Moore, personal communication, October 27, 2017.

that it is the ill person who dictates how much talk there is about death and dying, even if the well partner wants to speak more fully about her fears of a bad outcome or of being left to parent alone. If one partner wants to talk about death, while the other only wants to stay positive, a therapist can ask, "Knowing that you have different styles of coping, would it be OK to have a separate conversation with another therapist, or family member, about your worries?" The couple therapist may also try to normalize the fear that talking about death is disloyal to a hopeful perspective, or that talking about death hastens its approach.

There are several factors that can either complicate or ease this stage of life. Sometimes a couple has handled a smaller version of dependency or illness in early years, and they can draw on what they learned about each other and themselves from those experiences.

Jane (75) and Ted (85) faced her metastatic breast cancer and limited time ahead, after experiencing his bypass surgery a decade earlier. They recall how important it was for Ted to spend time alone and for Jane to confide her feelings to a small group of friends. Now, when he wants to close the door and meditate, she knows not to misconstrue that response as one of withdrawal, but instead sees him as trying to keep his equilibrium in the face of heartache.

When the couple can draw on a history of feeling mutually cared for and loved, the illness is a continuation of what has been present in the relationship all along. This is not to suggest that comforting each other and talking about illness will be a seamless process, but if there is a bedrock of love, this interpersonal intimacy will certainly help. Perhaps not surprisingly, however, it is the very relationships that were close, supportive, and dependent that are associated with an increased risk of complicated grief after the spouse dies (Lobb et al., 2010). Those who rated marriage as less satisfying and more conflicted seem to experience lower levels of depression and less decline in positive emotion after the death of a spouse than those who enjoyed a more intimate marriage (Prigerson et al., 2000; Bonanno et al., 2002; Ong et al., 2010). In many instances, the happier the marriage, the greater the sadness for the bereaved.

Secrets, separation, and high conflict make problems for any marriage but become particularly difficult during the end-of-life stage. A secret held between the couple for years may require special attention if it involves a third person. The secret may be about the genetics of a child who thought he was biologically related to both parents but is not, or the existence of a never-discussed sibling, or of a bankruptcy or mental illness, not previously shared because of shame. As death approaches, the couple may disagree about whether or not the secret should be disclosed with time to discuss it, or carried beyond the grave in perpetual silence. Sometimes, the secret is about an affair or about sexual orientation, or both.

Harold and Charlotte had been married for 50 years, and during most of their marriage, Harold had had a longstanding romantic relationship with another man. Charlotte had discovered Harold in bed with his lover many decades before and had decided to stay in the marriage and to never speak about this secret to anyone. Years later, when Harold was diagnosed with ALS, Charlotte wanted Harold to tell their son this secret before he died. In her caretaking of Harold during his illness, she had relinquished her bitterness about his affair, and she had felt closer to him. She felt deep sadness for both of them and all that they had sacrificed in order to protect Harold's secret. She wanted to tell their son and feel some release, but Harold protested, trying to extract a promise that she would never tell him. He feared his son's disapproval of him for having led a double life, and he imagined that his son would judge him with the same homophobia he judged himself.

In couple therapy, we discussed the burden that holding this information had placed on Charlotte, and the likelihood that their son already had some knowledge of this affair. Still, Harold was reluctant to share the truth about his sexual orientation. Then, one week when they came to therapy, Charlotte reported that their grandson, Miles, age 16, had confided in her that he was gay and was scared to tell his parents. I suggested to Harold that, by sharing the information about his own sexual orientation and by telling his family what a toll keeping this secret has taken on him and Charlotte, he could offer a powerful legacy to his family and interrupt the transmission of another family member having to live in secrecy. Harold died before this conversation occurred, but Charlotte felt she had received his blessing to talk to her son and grandson about his sexual orientation.

In addition to secrets, another tricky situation to navigate at the end of life is a couple's decision to separate, made just before the discovery of a terminal diagnosis. One woman who had decided to leave, reconsidered and moved back in, primarily to protect her young adult daughter from having to shoulder the responsibility of taking care of her father.

Another separating couple chose to live on different floors of a house as a temporary arrangement. When the terminal illness turned out to be chronic, the husband who had wanted to leave felt stuck. He had put his wishes on hold for several years and felt guilty about leaving, but resentful about staying with a partner whose end of life was not imminent. When the relationship has been volatile and abusive, it is preferable to follow through on the separation. A terminally ill person will not benefit from depending on a partner who is not dependable.

Legacy

Thinking together about what the dying spouse wants to leave behind is an important part of preparing for the end of life. Spouses may want to discuss putting aside funds for a charity or an organization that has been meaningful to them, or starting a scholarship in memory of the dying spouse. Couples may want to tell their shared stories on film or by writing down memories about their relationship that they want remembered by the remaining spouse and other family members. Other ideas include writing a list of annotated books and films that can be read and watched in the future, or compiling a collection of family recipes that can be made at future holidays and family gatherings.

If the dying partner has children, he or she may want to write letters that can be opened in the future at particular milestones, like a son's wedding day, or at the birth of a grandchild. One of the biggest gifts a dying partner can offer is a vote of confidence that the living partner will be able to carry on and raise the children well.[6] A therapist can help the ill parent articulate what values, information, and knowledge he or she wants to make sure get honored and passed along once he or she is gone. Here are some questions that can help facilitate a conversation about legacy issues:

- "What about you as a parent do you want to have carried forward?"
- "What do you know about your kids that is important for others to know that should be passed along to the extended family and to your partner?"

---

[6] Moore, personal communication October 27, 2017.

- "Are there objects, books, photos, or pieces of jewelry that you might want to designate for gifting to particular family members?"
- "Are there stories about your life about special days, lessons learned, and memories of other family members that you would like to write down so that they will be remembered?"

Final Words About Working with Couples at End-of-Life

As I think back over my career as a couple therapist, I am struck by how many fewer couples I have seen at this stage of life than at each of the others. In part, this could be function of how specialized end-of-life work has become. That is, there are grief counselors, palliative care and hospice specialists, and social workers assigned to a medical unit, all trained to work with end-of-life issues. But, it is also true that I have not sought out this work, largely because I expected it to be so challenging and painful. Dr. Rauch offered this advice to clinicians who, like me, might feel uncertain or anxious about engaging with patients who are dying: "People are so grateful to work with a clinician who isn't over-whelmed by this and can be curious." In other words, when a therapist can bring a stance of openness, inquisitiveness, and empathy to patients who are facing death, this therapeutic stance will go a long way, even if a therapist does not have years of experience or specialized training in end-of-life issues.

Therapists who choose to work with couples at the end of life often regard this work as deeply meaningful and rewarding. As Dr. Rosenberg explained during an interview at MGH:

> Our culture devalues aging and illness. Some people would say, "What's the point of couples therapy at the end of life?" I think it's deeply generative. One gets to help couples through recon-sideration of their identity and legacy. It's way beyond material attainment and instead about being able to connect with others and think about one's life. It's dignity work.

* *

I have seen couples over many decades as I have traversed the life cycle in my own marriage across most of the life stages explored in these pages. As a young wife, I often felt over my head seeing couples with children and like an imposter treating elderly couples. Now at a later stage, I wonder whether my younger patients think I do not remember what it was like to be a newlywed or to have a newborn. But knowledge about the common features of each life stage has helped me in my work with couples at different ages and stages. The life-cycle approach offers a map for therapists at any time of their lives to treat couples at stages not yet reached, or that exist in a distant rearview mirror. My hope is that this book will help couple therapists time-travel to where they need to be, regardless of their own life experience. As a couple therapist, I have had the opportunity to work with couples as they struggle and grow at every stage of development. Getting to witness and help guide couples through challenges that face us all, from dating to death, has been one of the greatest privileges of my career.

References

Addison, S. M., & Coolhart, D. (2015). Expanding the therapy paradigm with Queer couples: a relational intersectional lens. *Family Process, 54*(3), 435–453.

Administration on Aging. (2010). *A Profile of Older Americans: 2010.* Washington, DC: U.S. Department of Health and Human Services.

Ahrons, C. (2016). Divorce: An unscheduled family transition. In M. McGoldrick, N. G. Preto, & B. Carter (Eds.), *The Expanding Family Life Cycle: Individual, Family, and Social Perspectives* (5th ed., pp.376–393). Boston, MA: Pearson.

Albertini, M., & Kohli, M. (2009). What childless older people give: is the generational link broken? *Ageing and Society, 29*(8), 1261–1274.

Alzheimer's Foundation. (2011). *2011 Alzheimer's disease facts and figures.* Retrieved from http://alz.org/downloads/Facts_zheimer

Amato, P. R., & DeBoer, D. D. (2001). The transmission of marital instability across generations: relationship skills or commitment to marriage. *Journal of Marriage and Family, 63*(4), 1038–1051.

Amato, P. R., Booth, A., Johnson, D. R., & Rogers, S. J. (2007). *Alone together: How marriage in America is changing.* Cambridge, MA: Harvard University Press.

American Association of Retired Persons (AARP). (2010). *Sex, Romance, and Relationships: AARP Survey of midlife and older adults.* Retrieved from https://assets.aarp.org/rgcenter/general/srr_09.pdf

Arnett, J., & Fishel, E. (2013). *When will my grown-up kid grow up? Loving and understanding your emerging adult.* New York, NY: Workman Publishing.

Bacon, L. (1974). Early motherhood, accelerated role transition and social pathologies. *Social Forces, 52*(3), 333–341.

Barranti, C., & Cohen, H. (2000). Lesbian and gay elders: An invisible minority. In R. Schneider, N. Kropt, & A. Kisor, (Eds.), *Gerontological Social work: Knowledge, Service Settings, and Special Populations* (2nd ed., pp. 343–367). Belmont, CA: Wadworth.

Basson, R. (2000). The female sexual response: a different model. *Journal of Sex and Marital Therapy, 26*(1), 51–65.

Belsky, J., & Rovine, M. (1990). Patterns of marital change across the transition to parenthood. *Journal of Marriage and the Family, 52*, 109–123.

Ben-Ari, O. T., Findler, L., & Shlomo, S. B. (2013). When couples become grandparents: factors associated with the growth of each spouse. *Social Work Research, 37*(1), 26–36.

Benson, A. L., Silverstein, L. B., & Auerbach, C. F. (2005). From the margins to the center: gay fathers reconstruct the fathering role. *Journal of GLBT Family Studies, 1*(3), 1–29.

Bergman, K., Rubio, R. J., Green, R. J., & Padron, E. (2010). Gay men who become fathers via surrogacy: the transition to parenthood. *Journal of GLBT Family Studies, 6*(2), 111–141.

Birditt, K. S., Newton, N. J., Cranford, J. A., & Ryan, L. H. (2015). Stress and negative relationship quality among older couples: implications for blood pressure. *Journals of Gerontology Series B: Psychological Sciences and Social Sciences, 71*(5), 775–785.

Birditt, K. S., Newton, N. J., Cranford, J. A., & Webster, N. J. (2016). Chronic stress and negative marital quality among older couples: associations with waist circumference. *Journals of Gerontology Series B: Psychological Sciences and Social Sciences*, gbw112.

Bonanno, G. A., Wortman, C. B., Lehman, D. R., Tweed, R. G., Haring, M., Sonnega, J., & Nesse, R. M. (2002). Resilience to loss and chronic grief: a prospective study from preloss to 18-months postloss. *Journal of Personality & Social Psychology, 83*(5), 1150–1164.

Bookwala, J. (2012). Marriage and other partnered relationships in middle and late adulthood. In R. Blieszner & V. H. Bedford (Eds.), *Handbook of Aging and the Family* (2nd ed., pp. 91–124). Santa Barbara, CA: ABC-CLIO.

Booth, A., & Edwards, J. N. (1985). Age at marriage and marital instability. *Journal of Marital and Family Therapy, 47*, 67–75.

Bouchard, G. (2017). A dyadic examination of marital quality at the empty-nest phase. *The International Journal of Aging and Human Development*, pp. 1–17.

Bouchard, G., & McNair, J. L. (2016). Dyadic examination of the influence of family relationships on life satisfaction at the empty-nest stage. *Journal of Adult Development, 23*(3), 174–182.

Bradbury, T. N., & Karney, B. R. (2004). Understanding and altering the longitudinal course of marriage. *Journal of Marriage and the Family, 66*(4), 862–879.

Brim, O. G. (1992). *Ambition*. New York, NY: Basic Books.

Brim, O. G., Ryff, C. D., & Kessler, R. C. (Eds.). (2004). *How Healthy are we? A national study of well-being at midlife*. Chicago: University of Chicago Press.

Brotto, L. A., Bitzer, J., Laan, E., Leiblum, S., & Luria, M. (2010). Women's sexual desire and arousal disorders. *The Journal of Sexual Medicine, 7*(1 pt2), 586–614.

Brown, S. L., & Lin, I. F. (2012). The gray divorce revolution: rising divorce among middle-aged and older adults, 1990–2010. *Journal of Gerontology Series B: Psychological Sciences and Social Sciences, 67*(6), 731–741.

Brown, S. L., Bulanda, J. R., & Lee, G. R. (2012). Transition into and out of cohabitation in later life. *Journal of Marriage and Family*, *74*(4), 774–793.

Bryant, C. M., Taylor, R. J., Lincoln, K. D., Chatters, L. M., & Jackson, J. S. (2008). Marital satisfaction among African Americans and black Caribbeans: Findings from the national survey of American life. *Family Relations*, *57*(2), 239–253.

Busby, D., Carroll, J. S., & Willoughby, B. J. (2010). Compatibility or restraint? The effects of sexual timing on marriage relationships. *Journal of Family Psychology*, *24*(6), 766–774.

Cao, H., Mills-Koonce, R. W., Wood, C., & Fine, M. A. (2016). Identity transformation during the transition to parenthood among same-sex couples: an ecological, stress-strategy-adaptation perspective. *Journal of Family Theory & Review*, *8*(1), 30–59.

Carr, D., Boerner, K., & Moorman, S. M. (2013). End-of-life planning in a family context: does relationship quality affect whether (and with whom) older adults plan? *Journals of Gerontology Series B: Psychological Sciences and Social Sciences*, *68*(4), 586–592.

Carr, D., Freedman, V. A., Cornman, J. C., & Schwarz, N. (2014). Happy marriage, happy life? marital quality and subjective well-being in later life. *Journal of Marriage and Family*, *76*(5), 930–948.

Carrere, S., & Gottman, J. M. (1999). Predicting divorce among newlyweds from the first 3 minutes of a marital conflict discussion. *Family Process*, *38*(3), 293–301.

Carstensen, L. L., Gottman, J. M., & Levensen, R. W. (1995). Emotional behavior in long-term marriage. *Psychological Aging*, *10*(1), 140–149.

Carstensen, L. L., Isaacowitz, D. M., & Charles, S. T. (1999). Taking time seriously: a theory of socioemotional selectivity. *American Psychologist*, *54*(3), 165–181.

Carter, B., & McGoldrick, M. (Eds.). (1989). *The changing family life cycle: A framework for family therapy*, (2nd ed.). Needham, MA: Allyn and Bacon.

Cawood, H. H., & Bancroft, J. (1996). Steroid hormones, the menopause, sexuality and well-being of women. *Psychological Medicine*, *26*(5), 925–936.

Chambers, A., & Kravitz, A. (2011). Understanding the disproportionately low marriage rate among African Americans: an amalgam of sociological and psychological constraints. *Family Relations*, *60*(5), 648–660.

Charles, S. T., & Cartensen, L. L. (2009). Social and emotional aging. *Annual Review of Psychology*, *61*, 383–409.

Cherlin, A. J. (2014). American marriage in the early 21st Century. In A. Skolnick & J. H. Skolnick (Eds.), *Family in Transition, 17th Edition*. Boston, MA: Pearson.

Christensen, H. (1963). The timing of the first pregnancy as a factor in divorce: a cross-cultural analysis. *Eugenics Quarterly, 10*(3), 119–130.

Christensen, S. A., & Miller, R. B. (2006). Areas of desired change among married midlife individuals. *Journal of Couple and Relationship Therapy, 5*(3), 35–57.

Clausen, J. A. (1995). Gender, contexts, and turning points in adults' lives. In P. E. Moen, G. Elder, & K. Luscher (Eds.), *Examining Lives in Context: Perspectives on the Ecology of Human Development* (pp. 365–389). Washington, DC: American Psychological Association.

Coan, J. A., Schaefer, H. S., & Davidson, R. J. (2006). Social regulation of the neural response to threat. *Psychological Science, 17*(12), 1032–1039.

Cochran, S. D., Greer, J. S., & Mays, V. M. (2003). Prevalence of mental disorders, psychological distress, and mental services use among lesbian, gay, and bisexual adults in the United States. *Journal of Consulting and Clinical Psychology, 71*(1), 53–61.

Condie, S. J. (1989). Older married couples. In S. J. Bahr & E. T. Peterson (Eds.), *Aging and the Family*. Lexington, MA: D.C. Heath and Co.

Copen, C. E., Daniels, K., & Mosher, W. D. (2013). First premarital cohabitation in the United States: 2006–2010 National Survey of Family Growth. *National Health Statistics Reports, 64*, 1–16.

Cowan, C. P., & Cowan P. A. (1990). The Pie. In J. Touliatos, B. F Perlmutter, & M. A Straus (Eds.), *Handbook of Family Measurement Techniques* (pp. 296–324). Chapel Hill, NC: Carolina Population Center.

Cowan, C. P., & Cowan, P. A. (1995). Intervention to ease the transition to parenthood: why they are needed and what they can do. *Family Relations, 44*, 412–423.

Cowan, C. P., & Cowan, P. A. (1999). *When Partners Become Parents: The Big Life Change for Couples*, Revised Edition. New York, NY: Routledge.

Coyne, J. C., Rohrbaugh, M. J., Shoham, V., Sonnega, J. S., Nicklas, J. M., & Cranford, J. A. (2001). Prognostic importance of marital quality for survival of congestive heart failure. *The American Journal of Cardiology, 88*(5), 526–529.

Craig, L., & Bittman, M. (2005). The effects of children on adults' time-use: analysis of the incremental time costs of children in Australia. *Social Policy Research Centre, 143*, 1–37.

Crohan, S. E. (1996). Marital quality and conflict across the transition to parenthood in African-American and White couples. *Journal of Marriage and the Family, 58*, 933–944.

Curran, M., Hazen, N., Jacobvitz, D., Feldman, A., & Sasaki, T. (2006). How representations of the parental marriage predict marital emotional attunement during the transition to parenthood. *Journal of Family Psychology, 20*(3), 477–484.

Cutrona, C. E., Burzette, D. W., Wesner, R. G., Bryant, K. A., & Chalandra, M. (2011). Predicting relationship stability among midlife African American couples. *Journal of Consulting and Clinical Psychology*, *79*(6), 814–825.

D'Augelli, A. R., Rendina, H. J., Grossman, A. H., & Sinclair, K. O. (2007). Lesbian and gay youths' aspirations for marriage and raising children. *Journal of LGBT Issues in Counseling*, *1*(4), 77–98.

Davis, S. D., Lebow, J. L., & Sprenkle, D. H. (2012). Common factors of change in couple therapy. *Behavior Therapy*, *43*(1), 36–48

Dawber, T. R. (1980). *The Framingham study*. Cambridge MA: Harvard University Press.

Delamater, J. (2012). Sexual expression in later life: a review and synthesis. *Journal of Sex Research*, *49*(2–3), 125–141.

Delamater, J., & Koepsel, E. (2015). Relationships and sexual expression in later life: a biopsychosocial perspective. *Sexual and Relationship Therapy*, *30*(1), 37–59.

Delamater, J., & Sill, M. (2005). Sexual desire in later life. *Journal of Sex Research*, *42*(2), 138–149.

Dennerstein, L., Dudley, E., & Guthrie, J. (2002). Empty nest or revolving door? a retrospective study of women's quality of life in midlife during the phase of children leaving and re-entering the home. *Psychological Medicine*, *32*(3), 545–550.

DeOllos, I. Y., & Kapinus, C. A. (2002). Aging childless individuals and couples: suggestions for new directions in research. *Sociological Inquiry 72*(1), 72–80.

Doherty, W. J., Galston, W. A., Glenn, N. D., Gottman, J., Markey, B., Markman, H. J., Nock, S., & Wallerstein, J. (2002). *Why marriage matters: Twenty-one conclusions from the social sciences*. New York, NY: Institute for American Values.

Doss, B. D., Rhoades, G. K., Stanley, S. M., & Markman, H. J. (2009). The effect of the transition to parenthood on relationship quality: an 8-year prospective study. *Journal of Personality and Social Psychology*, *96*(3), 601–619.

Ducharme, J. K., & Kollar, M. M. (2012). Does the 'marriage benefit' extend to same-sex union? evidence from a sample of married lesbian couples in Massachusetts. *Journal of Homosexuality*, *59*(4), 580–591.

Dye, J. L. (2008). *Fertility of American Women: 2006*. Washington, DC: U.S. Census Bureau.

Earls, M. F. (2010). Incorporating recognition and management of perinatal and postpartum depression in pediatric practice. *Pediatrics*, *126*(5), pp. 1032–1039.

Elder, G. H., & Giele, J. Z. (Eds.). (2009). *The craft of life course research*. New York, NY: Guilford Press.

Erikson, E. (1951). *Childhood and society*. New York, NY: Norton.

Feinberg, M. E., Kan, M. L., & Goslin, M. C. (2009). Enhancing coparenting, parenting and child self-regulation: effects of family foundations 1 year after birth. *Prevention Science, 10*(3), 276–285.

Feldman, R., Sussman, A. L., & Zigler, E. (2004). Parental leave and work adaptation at the transition to parenthood: individual, marital, and social correlates. *Applied Developmental Psychology, 25*(4), 459–479.

Fishel, A. (1999). *Treating the adolescent in family therapy: A developmental and narrative approach.* Northvale, NJ: Jason Aronson.

Fishel, A. (2015). *Home for dinner: Mixing food, fun, and conversation for a happier family and healthier kids.* New York, NY: Amacom.

Fishel, A. (2016). Harnessing the power of family dinners to create change in family therapy. *Australian and New Zealand Journal of Family Therapy, 37*(4), 514–527.

Fishel, A., Feldman, E., Zuckerman, F., McSheffrey, C., & Wittman, C. (2011). First-time IVF couples making the transition to parenthood. *National Council on Family Relations Report,* Summer, 19–22.

Fisher, H. (2004). *Why we love: The nature and chemistry of love.* New York, NY: Holt and Co.

Friedman, H. S., & Martin, L. R. (2011). *The longevity project.* New York, NY: Hudson Street Press.

Frisco, M. L., & Williams, K. L. (2003). Perceived housework equity, marital happiness, and divorce in dual-earner households. *Journal of Family Issues, 23,* 51–73.

Fry, R., & Passel, J. S. (2014). In post-recession era, young adults drive continuing rise in multigenerational living," *Pew Research Reports,* July 17. Retrieved from https://web.archive.org/web/20150905053547/http://www.pewsocialtrends. org/2014/07/17/in-post-recession-era-young-adults-drive-continuing-rise-in-multi-generational-living/

Fuller-Thomson, E., & Minkler, M. (2001). American grandparents providing extensive childcare to their grandchildren: prevalence and profile. *The Gerontologist, 41*(2), 201–209.

Fung, H. H., & Carstensen, L. L. (2006). Goals change when life's fragility is primed: lessons learned from older adults, the September 11 attacks, and SARS. *Social Cognition, 24*(3), 248–78.

Fung, H. H., Carstensen, L. L., & Lang, F. R. (2001). Age-related patterns in social networks among European Americans and African Americans: implications for socioemotional selectivity across the life span. *International Journal of Aging Human Development, 52*(3), 185–206.

Gartrell, N., Banks, A., Reed, N., Hamilton, J., Rodas, C., & Deck, A. (2000). The National lesbian Family Study: 3. Interviews with mothers of five-year-olds. *American Journal of Orthopsychiatry, 70*(4), 542–548.

Gates, G. J. (2015). Marriage and family: LGBT individuals and same-sex couples. *Future of Children, 25*(2), 67–87. Retrieved from http://princeton.edu/futureofchildren/publications/docs/MarriageandFamily.pdf

Gawande, A. (2014). *Being mortal: Medicine and what matters in the end.* New York, NY: Metropolitan Books.

Generous, M. A., & Keeley, M. (2017). Wished for and avoided conversation with terminally ill individuals during final conversations. *Death Studies, 41*(3), 162–172.

Gherdingen, D. K., & Chaloner, K. (1994). Mothers' experience with household roles and social support during the first postpartum year. *Women and Health, 21*(4), 57–74.

Glenn, N. D. (1989). Duration of marriage, family composition, and marital happiness. *National Journal of Sociology, 3*(1), 3–24.

Goldberg, A. E., & Perry-Jenkins, M. (2004). Division of labor and working-class women's well being across the transition to parenthood. *Journal of Family Psychology, 18*(1), 225–236.

Goldberg, A. (2010). *Lesbian and gay parents and their children: Research on the family life cycle.* Washington, DC: American Psychological Association.

Goldberg, A. E, & Smith, J. Z. (2011). Stigma, social context, and mental health: lesbian and gay couples across the transition to adoptive parenthood. *Journal of Counseling Psychology 58*(1), 139–150.

Goldberg, A. E., & Perry-Jenkins, M. (2007). The division of labor and perceptions of parental roles: lesbian couples across the transition to parenthood. *Journal of Social and Personal Relationships, 24*(2), 297–318.

Goldberg, A. E., & Smith, J. Z. (2008). The social context of lesbian mothers' anxiety during early parenthood. *Parenting: Science & Practice, 8*(3), 213–239.

Goldberg, A. E., Kashy, D., & Smith, J. Z. (2012). Gender-typed play behavior in early childhood: adopted children with lesbian, gay, and heterosexual parents. *Sex Roles, 67*(9–10), 503–515.

Goldsen, J., Bryan, A. E. B., Kim, H. J., Muraco, A., Jen, S., & Fredricksen-Goldsen, K. I. (2017). Who says I do: the changing context of marriage and health and quality of life for LGBT older adults. *The Gerontologist, 57*(S1), 50–62.

Golumbok, S., Mellish, L., Jennings, S., Casey, P., Tasker, F., & Lamb, M. E. (2014). Adoptive gay father families: parent-child relationships and children's psychological adjustment. *Child Development, 85*(2), 456–468.

Gomez, R. G., & Madey, S. F. (2001). Coping-with-hearing-loss model for older adults. *Journal of Gerontology: Series B: Psychological Sciences 56B*(4), P223–P225.

Goodman, J. H. (2004). Paternal postpartum depression, its relationship to maternal postpartum depression, and implications for family health. *Journal of Advanced Nursing, 45*(1), 26–35.

Gorschoff, S. M., John, O. P., & Helson, R. (2008). Contextualizing change in marital satisfaction during middle age: an 18-year longitudinal study. *Psychological Science, 19*(11), 1194–1200.

Gott, M., & Hinchliff, S. (2003). How important is sex in later life? the views of older people. *Social Science and Medicine, 56*(8), 1617–1628.

Gottman J. M., Coan, J., Carrere, S., & Swanson, C. (1998). Predicting marital happiness and stability from newlywed interactions. *Journal of Marriage and Family, 60*, 5–22.

Gottman, J. M. (1999). *A scientifically-based marital therapy: Clinician's manual.* Seattle, WA: The Gottman's Institute.

Gottman, J. M., & Gottman, J. S. (2007). *And baby makes three.* New York, NY: Crown.

Gottman, J. M., & Levensen, R. W. (2000). The timing of divorce: predicting when a couple will divorce over a 14-year period. *Journal of Marriage and Family, 62*(3), 737–745.

Gottman, J. M., & Levensen, R. W. (2002). A two-factor model for predicting when a couple will divorce: exploratory analyses using 14-year longitudinal data. *Family Process, 41*(1), 83–96.

Gottman, J. M., & Silver, N. (2016). *The seven principles for making marriage work.* New York, NY: Random House.

Green, R. J., & Mitchell, V. (2015). Gay, lesbian, and bisexual issues in couple's therapy. In A.S. Gurman, J. L. Lebow, & D. K. Snyder (Eds.), *Clinical Handbook of Couples Therapy* (5th ed.). New York, NY: Guilford.

Grote, N. K., & Clark, M. S. (2001). Perceiving unfairness in the family: cause or consequence of marital distress? *Journal of Personality and Social Psychology, 80*(2), 281–293.

Hagen, J. D., & DeVries, H. M. (2004). Marital satisfaction at the empty-nest phase of the family life cycle: a longitudinal study. *Marriage and Family: A Christian Journal, 7*(1), 83–98.

Hagestad, G. O. (1988). Demographic change and the life course: some emerging trends in the family realm. *Family Relations 37*, 405–410.

Heatherington, E. M., & Kelly, J. (2002). *For better or for worse: Divorce reconsidered.* New York, NY: W.W. Norton.

Henry, R. G., & Miller, R. B. (2004). Marital problems occurring in midlife: implications for couples therapists. *The American Journal of Family Therapy, 32*(5), 405–417.

Hepworth, J., Ryder, R. G., & Dreyer, A. S. (1984). The effects of parental loss on the formation of intimate relationships. *Journal of Marital and Family Therapy, 10*(1), 73–82.

Hirayama, R., & Walker, A. J. (2011). When a partner has a sexual problem: gendered implications for psychological well-being in later life. *The Journals of Gerontology: Series B, 66B*(6), 804–813.

Holter, H., Anderheim, L., Bergh, C., & Moller, A. (2006). First IVF treatment: short term impact on psychological well-being and the marital relationship. *Human Reproduction, 21*(12), 3295–3302.

Holt-Lunstad, J., Smith, T. B., & Layton, J. B. (2010). Social relationships and mortality risk: a meta-analytic review. *PLoS Med, 7*(7), e1000316.

Hostetler, A. J. (2013). Sexual orientation, middle adulthood, and narratives of transition and change. In C.J. Patterson & A. R. D'Augelli (Eds.), *Handbook of psychology and sexual orientation*. New York, NY: Oxford University Press.

House, J., Landis, K., & Umberson, D. (1988). Social relationships and health. *Science,* 241(4865), 540–545.

Huang, A. J., Subak, L. L., Thom, D. H., Van Den Eeden, S. K., Ragins, A. L., Kupperman, M., Shen, H., & Brown, J. S. (2009). Sexual function and aging in racially and ethnically diverse women. *Journal of American Geriatric Society,* 57(8), 1362–1368.

Huston, T. L., & Vangelisti, A. L. (1995). How parenthood affects marriage. In M.A. Fitzpatrick & A.L. Vangelisti, (Eds.), *Explaining marital interactions* (pp. 147–176). Thousand Oaks, CA: Sage Publications.

Hymowitz, K., Carroll, J. S., Wilcox, W. B., & Kaye, K. (2013). Knot yet: The benefits and costs of delayed marriage in America. The National Marriage Project at the University of Virginia, The National Campaign to Prevent Teen and Unplanned Pregnancy and The Relate Institute, 1–40. Retrieved from http://nationalmarriageproject.org/wp-content/uploads/2013/03/KnotYet-FinalForWeb.pdf

Institute of Medicine (2011). *The health of lesbian, gay, bisexual, and transgender people: Building a foundation for better understanding.* Washington, DC: National Academies Press.

Isaacs, M. R. (2006). *Maternal depression: The silent epidemic in poor communities.* Baltimore: Annie E. Casey Foundation.

Jacobson, N., & Gottman, J. (2007). *When men batter women.* New York, NY: Simon and Schuster.

Jensen, T. M., & Bowen, G. L. (2015). Mid and late-life divorce and parents' perceptions of emerging adult children's emotional reactions. *Journal of Divorce and Remarriage, 56*(5), 409–427.

Jose, A. K., O'Leary, D., & Moyer, A. (2010). Does premarital cohabitation predict subsequent marital stability and marital quality? a meta-analysis. *Journal of Marriage and Family, 72*(1), 105–116.

Jung, C. G. (2001). *Modern man in search of a soul.* New York, NY: Routledge Classics.

Kamp Dush, C. M., & Amato, P. R. (2005). Consequences of relationship status and quality for subjective well-being. *Journal of Social and Personal Relationships, 22*(5), 607–627.

Kamp Dush, C. M., & Taylor, M. G. (2012). Trajectories of marital conflict across the life course: predictors and interactions with marital happiness trajectories. *Journal of Family Issues, 33*(3), 341–368.

Kaufman, G., & Elder, G. H. (2003). Grandparenting and age identity. *Journal of Aging Studies, 17*(3), 269–282.

Keeley, M. P., & Generous, M. A. (2017). Final conversations: Overview and practical implications for patients, families, and healthcare workers. *Behavioral Sciences, 7*(2), 17–26.

Keizer, R., Dykstra, P. A., & Jansen, M. D. (2008). Pathways into childlessness: evidence of gendered life course dynamics. *Journal of Biosocial Science, 40*(6), 863–878.

Kennedy, S., & Ruggles, S. (2014). Breaking up is hard to count: the rise of divorce in the United States, 1980–2010. *Demography, 51*(2), 587–598.

Kim, H. J., & Fredriksen-Goldsen, K. I. (2016). Living arrangement and loneliness among lesbian, gay, and bisexual older adults. *The Gerontologist, 56*, 548–558.

King, K. B., Reis, H. T., Porter, L. A., & Norsen, L. H. (1993). Social support and long-term recovery from coronary artery surgery: effects on patients and spouses. *Health Psychology, 12*(1), 56–63.

Kluwer, E. (2010). From partnership to parenthood. *Journal of Family Theory and Review, 2*(2), 105–125.

Kluwer, E., & Johnson, M. D. (2007). Conflict frequency and relationship quality across the transition to parenthood. *Journal of Marriage and Family, 69*(5), 1089–1106.

Kluwer, E., Heesink, J. A. M., & Van de Vliert, E. (1996). Marital conflict over the division of household labor and paid work. *Journal of Marriage and the Family, 58*, 958–969.

Kobrin, F. E., & Waite, L. J. (1984). Effects of childhood family structure on the transition to marriage. *Journal of Marriage and Family, 4*, 807–816.

Koropeckyj-Cox, T., Pienta, A. M., & Brown, T. H. (2007). Women of the 1950s and the "normative" life course: The implications of childlessness, fertility timing, and marital status for psychological well-being in late midlife. *International Journal of Aging and Human Development, 64*(4), 299–330.

Krychman, M. (2007). Vaginal atrophy: the 21st century health issue affecting quality of life. *Medscape Ob/Gyn and Women's Health*. Retrieved from http://medscape.com/viewarticle/561934

Lannutti, P. J. (2010). Security, recognition, and misgivings: exploring older same-sex couples' experiences of legally recognized same-sex marriage. *Journal of Social and Personal Relationships, 28*(1), 64–82.

Laumann, E. O., Das, A., & Waite, L. J. (2008). Sexual dysfunction among older adults: prevalence and risk factors from a nationally representative US probability sample of men and women 57 to 85 years of age. *Journal of Sex Medicine, 5*(10), 2300–2311.

Laumann, E. O., Gagnon, J. H., Michael, R. T., & Michaels, S. (1994). *The social organization of sexuality: Sexual practices in the United States*. Chicago: University of Chicago Press.

Laumann, E. O., Paik, A. M. A., & Rosen, R. C. (1999). Sexual dysfunction in the United States: prevalence and predictors. *Journal of the American Medical Association, 281*(6), 537–544.

Lawrence, E., Nylen, K., & Cobb, R. J. (2007). Prenatal expectations and marital satisfaction over the transition to parenthood. *Journal of Family Psychology, 21*(2),155–154.

Lee, G. R., & Bulanda, J. R. (2005). Change and consistency in the relation of marital status to personal happiness. *Marriage and Family Review, 38*(1), 69–84.

Lee, G. R., & Payne, K. K. (2010). Changing marriage patterns since 1970: what's going on, and why? *Journal of Comparative Family Studies, 41*, 537–555.

Levensen, R. W., Carstensen, L. L., & Gottman, J. M. (1993). Long-term marriages: age, gender, and satisfaction. *Psychology and Aging, 8*(2), 301–313.

Levensen, R. W., Carstensen, L. L., & Gottman, J.M. (1994). Influence of age and gender on affect, physiology, and their interrelations: a study of long-term marriages. *Journal of Personality and Social Psychology, 67*(1), 56–68.

Levinson, D. J. (1978). *Seasons of a man's life*. New York, NY: Knopf.

Lewis, C. S. (1994). *A grief observed*. New York, NY: Harper Collins.

Lieblum, S. R., Aviv, A., & Hammer, H. (1998). Life after infertility treatment: a long-term investigation of marital and sexual satisfaction. *Human Reproduction, 13*(12), 3569–3574.

Lin, I. F., & Brown, S. L. (2012). Unmarried boomers confront old age: a national portrait. *The Gerontologist, 52*(2), 153–165.

Lindau, S. T., Schumm, M. A., Laumann, E. O., Levinson, W. O., Muircheartaigh, C. A., & Waite, L. J. (2007) A study of sexuality and health among older adults in the United States. *New England Journal of Medicine, 357*(8), 762–74.

Livingston, G. (2014). Growing number of dads home with the kids. *Pew Research Reports*. Retrieved from http://web.archive.org/web/20150905055233/http://pewsocialtrends.org/2014/06/05/growing-number-of-dads-home-with-the-kids/

Lobb, E. A., Kristjanson, L. J., Aoun, S. M., Monterosso, L., Halkett, G., & Davies, A. (2010). Predictors of complicated grief: a systematic review of empirical studies. *Death Studies, 34*(8), 673–698.

Lodge, A., & Umberson, D. (2012). All shook up: sexuality in mid-to-later-life married couples. *Journal of Marriage and Family, 74*(3), 428–443.

Lyness, K. P. (2012). Therapeutic considerations in same-sex divorce. In J. Bigner & J. Wetchler (Eds.), *Handbook of LGBT-affirmative couple and family therapy* (pp. 377–391). New York, NY: Routledge.

MacKey, R. A., Diemer, M. A., & O'Brien, B. A. (2004). Relational factors in understanding satisfaction in the lasting relationships of heterosexual and same-sex couples. *Journal of Homosexuality, 47*(1), 111–36.

Markman, H. J., Rhoades, G. K., Stanley, S. M., & Ragan, E. P. (2010). The premarital communication roots of marital distress and divorce: the first five years of marriage. *Journal of Family Psychology, 24*, 289–298.

Marks, N. F., Bumpass, L. L., & Jun, H. (2004). Family roles and well-being during the middle life course. In O. G. Brim, C. D. Ryff, & R. C. Kessler (Eds.), *How healthy are we? A national study of well-being at midlife.* Chicago: University of Chicago.

Martin, S. (2004). *Growing evidence for a 'divorce divide?' Education and marital dissolution rates in the US since the 1970s. Working Paper on social dimensions of inequality.* New York, NY: Russell Sage Foundation.

McDaniel, S., Hepworth, J., & Doherty, W.J. (2009). *The shared experience of illness: Stories of patients, families, and their therapists.* New York, NY: Behavioral Science.

McGoldrick, M., Carter, B., & Preto, N. G. (2016). *The expanding family life cycle: individual, family, and social perspectives* (5th ed.). Boston, MA: Pearson.

McKinnon, J. (2003). *The black population in the United States: March 2002.* Current Population Reports, Series P20-541. Washington, DC: Bureau of the Census.

McPherson, D. (1993). Gay parenting couples: Parenting arrangements, arrangement satisfaction, and relationship satisfaction, Unpublished doctoral dissertation, Pacific Graduate School of Psychology, Palo Alto, CA.

Mitchell, B. A., & Wister, A. V. (2015). Midlife challenge or welcome departure? cultural and family-related expectations of empty nest transitions. *The International Journal of Aging and Human Development, 81*(4), 260–80.

Moore, C. W., & Rauch, P. K. (2015). Addressing the needs of children when a parent has cancer. In J. C. Holland, W. S. Breitbart, P. N. Butow, P. B. Jacobsen, M. J. Loscalzo, & R. McCorkle (Eds.), *Psycho-oncology,* (3rd ed., pp. 579–584). New York, NY: Oxford University Press.

Moore, C. W., & Rauch, P. K. (2017). Communicating with children when a parent is dying. In D. W. Kissane, B. D. Bultz, P. N. Butow, C. L. Bylund, S. Noble, & S. Wilkinson (Eds.), *Oxford textbook of communication in oncology and palliative care.* New York, NY: Oxford University Press.

Moore, C. W., & Rauch, P. K. (2017). Parental cancer. In D. Morley, X. Li, & C. Jenkinson (Eds.), *Children and young people's response to parental illness* (pp. 106–129). Boca Raton: CRC Press, Taylor and Francis.

Mroczek, D. K., & Almeida, D. M. (2004). The effect of daily stress, personality, and age on daily negative affect. *Journal of Personality, 72*(2), 355–378.

National Institute on Aging. (2007). *Living long & well in the 21st Century: Strategic directions for research on aging* (Pub. No. 07-6252). Washington, DC: National Institutes of Health.

Neugarten, B. (1979). Time, age, and the life-cycle. *The American Journal of Psychiatry, 136,* 887–894.

Nomaguchi, K. M., & Milkie, M. (2003). Costs and rewards of children: The effects of becoming a parent on adults' lives. *Journal of Marriage and Family, 66,* 413–430.

Obergefell v. Hodges. (2015). No. 14–556, slip op. at 23 (U.S. June 26, 2015).

Olson, D. H., & Olson, A. K. (1999). PREPARE/ENRICH Program: Version 2000. In R. Berger & M.T. Hannah (Eds.), *Preventive approaches in couples therapy.* Philadelphia PA, Brunner/Mazel.

Ong, A. D., Fuller-Rowell, T. E., & Bonanno, G. A. (2010). Prospective predictors of positive emotions following spousal loss. *Psychology & Aging, 25*(3), 653–660.

Orth-Gomer, K., Wamala, S. P., Horsten, M., Schenck-Gustafsson, K., Schneiderman, N., & Mittleman. M. A. (2000). Marital stress worsens prognosis in women with coronary heart disease. *Journal of the American Medical Association, 284,* 3008–14.

Osborne, R. S. (2003). Percentage of Childless Women 40 to 44 Years Old Increases Since 1976, Census Bureau Reports. U.S. Census Bureau Press Release.

Otis, M. D., Rostosky, S. S., Riggle, E. D., & Hamrin, R. (2006). Stress and relationship quality in same-sex couples. *Journal of Social and Personal Relationships, 23*(1), 81–99.

Papernow, P. (2013). *Surviving and thriving in stepfamily relationships: What works and what doesn't.* New York, NY: Routledge.

Papernow, P. (2017). Recoupling in mid-life and beyond: from love at last to not so fast. *Family Process.* Retrieved from http://onlinelibrary.wiley.com.ezp-prod1.hul.harvard.edu/doi/10.1111/famp.12315/full

Papini, D. R., & Roggman, L. A. (1993). Parental attachment to early adolescents' and parents' emotional and marital adjustment: a longitudinal study. *Journal of Early Adolescence, 13*(3), 311–328.

Parker, P. (2016). Facts about American fathers. *Pew Research Reports.* Retrieved from http://pewresearch.org/fact-tank/2016/06/16/fathers-day-facts.

Pasley, K., & Lee, M. (2010). Stress and coping in the context of stepfamily life. In C. Price & S. H. Price (Eds.), *Family and change: Coping with stressful life events* (3rd ed., pp. 223–259). Thousand Oaks, CA: Sage.

Patterson, C. J. (2006). Children of lesbian and gay parents. *Current Directions in Psychological Science, 15*(5), 241–244.

Person, E. S. (1989). *Dreams of love and fateful encounters.* New York, NY: Norton.

Petch, J., & Halford, W. K. (2008). Psycho-education to enhance couples' transition to parenthood. *Clinical Psychology Review, 28*(7), 1125–1137.

Pew Research Center (2013). Fact Tank news in the numbers. Retrieved from http://pewresearch.org/fact-tank/2017/04/06/number-of-u-s-adults-cohabiting-with-a-partner-continues-to-rise-especially-among-those-50-and-older/

Pew Research Center (2013). *Social and demographic trends: A rising share of young adults live in their parents' home.* Washington, DC.

Pew Research Center (2015). Rise in dual income households. http://pewresearch.org/ft_dual-income-households-1960-2012-2/ (Accessed on 2/6/18).

Pew Research Center (2016). Number of adults cohabitating with a partner continues to rise, especially among those 50 and older. Retrieved from http://pewresearch.org/fact-tank/2017/04/06/number-of-u-s-adults-cohabiting-with-a-partner-continues-to-rise-especially-among-those-50-and-older/

Pew Research Center (2017). Intermarriage in the US 50 years after Loving v. Virginia. Retrieved from http://pewsocialtrends.org/2017/05/18/inter-marriage-in-the-u-s-50-years-after-loving-v-virginia/.

Piaget, J., & Inhelder, B. (1969). *The psychology of the child* (2nd ed.). New York, NY: Basic Books.

Pinderhughes, E. B. (2002). African American marriage in the 20th century. *Family Process, 41*(2), 268–282.

Pinsof, W. M. (2002). The death of "till death do us part: the transformation of pair-bonding in the 20th century. *Family Process, 4*(2), 135–157.

Pittman, F. (1990). *Private lies: Infidelity and the betrayal of intimacy.* New York, NY: W.W. Norton.

Prigerson, H. G., Maciejewski, P. K., & Rosenheck, R. A. (2000). Preliminary explorations of the harmful interactive effects of widowhood and marital harmony on health, health service use, and health care costs. *The Gerontologist, 40*(3), 349–357.

Proulx, C. M., & Synder-Rivas, L. A. (2013). The longitudinal associations between marital happiness, problems, and self-rated health. *Journal of Family Psychology, 27*(2), 194–205.

Pudrovska, T. (2008). Psychological implications of motherhood and fatherhood in midlife: Evidence from sibling models. *Journal of Marriage and Family, 70*(1), 168–181.

Quam, J. K., Whitford, G. S., Dziengel, L. E., & Knochel, K. A. (2010). Exploring the nature of same-sex relationships. *Journal of Gerontological Social Work*, *53*(8), 702–722.

Rastogi, M., & Thomas, V. K. (2008). *Multicultural couple therapy*. Thousand Oaks, CA: Sage Publications.

Rauch, P. K., & Muriel, A. C. (2006). *Raising an emotionally healthy child when a parent is sick*. New York, NY: McGraw Hill.

Reitzes, D. C., & Mutran, E. J. (2004). Grandparenthood: factors influencing frequency of grandparent-grandchildren contact and grandparent role satisfaction. *The Journal of Gerontology Series B-Psychological Sciences and Social Sciences*, *59B*(1), S9–S16.

Riggle, E. D., Rostosky, S. S., & Horne, S. G. (2010). Psychological distress, well-being, and legal recognition in same-sex couple relationships. *Journal of Family Psychology*, *24*(1), 82–86.

Robbles, T. F., Slatcher, R. B., Trombello, J. M., & McGinn, M. M. (2014). Marital quality and health: a meta-analytic review. *Psychological Bulletin*, *140*(1), 140–187.

Rogge, R. D., & Bradbury, T. N. (1999). Till violence does us part: the differing roles of communication and aggression in predicting adverse marital outcomes. *Journal of Consulting and Clinical Psychology*, *67*(3), 340–351.

Rogge, R. M., & Bradbury, T. N. (1999). Recent advances in the prediction of marital outcomes. In R. Berger & M. T. Hannah (Eds.), *Preventive approaches in couples therapy*. Philadelphia, PA: Brunner Mazel.

Rolland, J. S. (1987). Chronic illness and the life cycle: a conceptual framework. *Family Process*, *26*(2), 203–221.

Ryder, R. (1970). Dimensions of early marriage. *Family Process*, *9*(1), 51–68.

Sassler, S., & Kamp Dush, C. M. (2009). The pace of relationship progression: does timing to sexual involvement matter? Paper presented at a National Center for Family and Marriage Research Conference, Bowling Green State University.

Sassler, S., Addo, F. R., & Lichter, D. T. (2012). The tempo of sexual activity and later relationship quality. *Journal of Marriage and Family*, *74*(4), 708–725.

Schacher, S. J., Auberbach, C. F., & Silverstein, L. B. (2005). Gay fathers expanding the possibilities for us all. *Journal of GLBT Family Studies*, *1*(3), 31–52.

Schulz, M. S., Cowan, C., & Cowan, P. (2006). Promoting healthy beginnings: a randomized controlled trial of a preventive intervention to preserve marital quality during the transition to parenthood. *Journal of Consulting and Clinical Psychology*, *74*(1), 20–31.

Sheehy, G. (1976). *Passages*. New York, NY: Dutton.

Skolnick, A. (2013). The life course revolution. In A. S. Skolnick & J.H. Skolnick (Eds.), *Family in transition* (17th ed., pp. 31–39). Boston, MA: Pearson.

Small, S. A., Cornelius, S., & Eastman, G. (1983). *Parenting adolescent children: A period of adult storm and stress?* Paper presented at the Ninety-First Annual Convention of the American Psychological Association, Anaheim, CA.

Sprenkle, D. H., & Blow, A. J. (2004). Common factors and our sacred models. *Journal of Marital and Family Therapy, 30*(2), 113–130.

Stanley, S. M., Rhoades, G. K., & Markman, H. J. (2006). Sliding vs. deciding: inertia and the pre-marital cohabitation effect. *Family Relations, 55*(4), 499–509.

Stanley, S. M., Rhoades, G. K., & Whitton, S. W. (2010). Commitment: functions, formation, and the securing of romantic attachment. *Journal of Family Theory and Review, 2*(4), 243–257.

Steinberg, L., & Silk, J. S. (2012). Parenting adolescents. In M. H. Bornstein (Eds.), *Handbook of Parenting, Vol. 1: Children and Parenting* (2nd ed.). New York, NY: Routledge.

Stemp, P. S., Turner, R. J., & Noh, S. (1986). Psychological distress in the postpartum period: the significance of social support. *Journal of Marriage and the Family, 48*, 271–277.

Stevenson, B., & Wolfers, J. (2007). Marriage and divorce: changes and their driving forces. *Journal of Economic Perspectives, 21*(2), 1–42.

Teachman, J. (2003). Premarital sex, premarital cohabitation, and the risk of subsequent marital dissolution among women. *Journal of Marriage and Family, 65*, 444–455.

Teachman, J. D., Tedrow, L. M., & Crowder, K. D. (2000). The changing demography of America's families. *Journal of Marriage and Family, 62*(4), 1234–1246.

Temel, J. S., Greer, J. A., Muzikansky, A., Gallagher, E. R., Admane, S., Jackson, V. A., Dahlin, C. M., Blinderman, C. D., Jacobsen, J., Pirl, W. F., Billings, J. A., & Lynch, T. J. (2010). Early palliative care for patients with metastatic non-small-cell lung cancer. *New England Journal of Medicine, 363*(8), 733–742.

Toman, W. (1993). *Family therapy and sibling position.* Northvale, NJ: Jason Aronson.

Trillin, C. (2006). *About Alice.* New York, NY: Random House.

Twenge, J. M., Campbell, W. K., & Foster, C. A. (2003). Parenthood and marital satisfaction: a meta-analytic review. *Journal of Marriage and Family, 65*(3), 574–583.

Umberson, D., Pudrovska, T., & Reczek, C. (2010). Parenthood, childlessness, and well-being: a life course perspective. *Journal of Marriage and the Family, 72*(3), 612–629.

Umberson, D., Williams, K., Powers, D. A., Liu, H., & Needham, B. (2006). You make me sick: marital quality and health over the life course. *Journal of Health and Social Behavior, 47*(1), 1–16.

United States Census Bureau. (2016). Retrieved from https://census.gov/hhes/socdemo/marriage/

United States Department of Labor (2011). Bureau of Labor Statistics. Employment and Earnings, Annual Averages, January.

U.S. Census Bureau. (2017). https://census.gov/data/tables/time-series/demo/families/marital.html (accessed 2/6/17).

Vaillant, G. E. (2012). *Triumphs of experience: The men of the Harvard Grant study.* Cambridge, MA: Harvard University Press.

Waite, L. J., & Gallagher, M. (2000). *The case for marriage: Why married people are happier, healthier, and better off financially.* New York, NY: Doubleday.

Waite, L. J., Laumann, E. O., Das, A., & Schumm, L. P. (2009). Sexuality: measure of partnerships, practices, attitudes, and problems in the National Social Life, Health, and Aging Project. *Journals of Gerontology: Social Sciences, 64B*(Suppl. 1), i56–i66.

Waldinger, R. J. (2010). What's love got to do with it? social functioning, perceived health, and daily happiness in married octogenarians. *Psychological Aging, 25*(2), 422–431.

Waldinger, R. J., & Schulz, M. S. (2016). The long reach of nurturing family environments: links with midlife emotion-regulatory styles and late-life security in intimate relationships. *Psychological Science, 27*(11), 1443–1450.

Waldinger, R. J., Cohen, S., Schulz, M., & Crowell, J. (2015). Security attachment to spouses in late life: concurrent and prospective links with cognitive and emotional well-being. *Clinical Psychological Science, 3*(4), 516–529.

Walker, R. B., & Luszcz, M. A. (2009). The health and relationship dynamics of late-life couples: a systematic review of the literature. *Aging and Society, 29*(3), 455–480.

Walsh, F. (2016). Applying a family resilience framework in training, practice, and research: mastering the art of the possible. *Family Process, 55*(4), 616–632.

Wang, W. (2015). The link between a college education and a lasting marriage. *Pew Research Report.* Retrieved from http://pewresearch.org/fact-tank/2015/12/04/education-and-marriage/

Weaver, K., Rowland, J., Alfano, C., & McNeel, T. (2010). Parental cancer and the family: a population-based estimate of the number of US cancer survivors residing with their minor children. *Cancer, 116*(18), 4395–4401.

Wenger, G. C., Dykstra, P. A., Melkas, T., & Knipscheer, K. C. P. M. (2007). Social embeddedness and late-life parenthood: community activity, close ties, and support networks. *Journal of Family Issues, 28*(11), 1419–1456.

Werner, E., & Smith, R. S. (2011). *Journeys from childhood to midlife: Risk, resilience, and recovery.* Ithaca, NY: Cornell University Press.

Wethington, E. (2000). Expecting stress: Americans and the "midlife crisis." *Motivation and Emotion, 24*(2), 85–103.

Whitaker, C., & Napier, A. (1977). *The family crucible.* New York, NY: Harper Collins.

White, L., & Edwards, J. N. (1990). Emptying the nest and parental well-being: an analysis of national panel data. *American Sociological Review, 55*(2), 235–242.

Whitton, S. W., Rhoades, G. K., Stanley, S. M., & Markman, H. J. (2008). Effects of parental divorce on marital commitment and confidence. *Journal of Family Psychology, 22*(5), 789–793.

Wienke, C., & Hill, G. J. (2009). Does the 'marriage benefit' extend to partners in gay and lesbian relationships? *Journal of Family Issues, 30*(2), 259–289.

Wight, R. G., LeBlanc, A. J., & Badgett, L. (2013). Same-sex legal marriage and psychological well-being: findings from the California Health Interview Survey. *American Journal of Public Health, 103*(2), 339–346.

Wight, R. G., Leblanc, A. J., de Vries, B., & Detels, R. (2012). Stress and mental health among midlife and older gay-identified men. *American Journal of Public Health, 102*(3), 503–510.

Williams, K. (2003). Has the future of marriage arrived? a contemporary examination of gender, marriage, and psychological well-being. *Journal of Health and Social Behavior, 44*(4), 470–87.

Williams, M. E., & Fredriksen-Goldsen, K. I. (2014). Same-sex partnerships and the health of older adults. *Journal of Community Psychology, 40*(5), 558–570.

Wright, A. A., Zhang, B., Ray, A., Mack, J. W., Trice, E., Balboni, T., Mitchell, S. L., Jackson, V. A., Block, S. D., Maciejewski, P. K., & Prigerson, H. G. (2008). Associations between end-of-life discussions, patient mental health, medical care near death, and caregiver bereavement adjustment. *Journal of the American Medical Association, 300*(14), 1665–73.

Yang, Y. (2008). Social inequalities in happiness in the United States, 1972–2004: an age-period-cohort analysis. *American Sociological Review, 73*(2), 204–226.

Zhang, X., & Hayward, M. (2001). Childlessness and the psychological well-being of older persons. *Journal of Gerontology Series B, 56*(5), S311–S320.

About the Author

Anne K. Fishel, PhD, is a family therapist, clinical psychologist, and Associate Clinical Professor of Psychology at the Harvard Medical School. She is Director of the Family and Couple Therapy Program at Massachusetts General Hospital, where she trains child and adult psychiatry residents, psychology interns, and social workers in family and couple therapy and has won many teaching prizes.

She is the author of two previous books: *Home for Dinner: Mixing Food, Fun, and Conversation for a Happier Family and Healthier Kids (2015)* and *Treating the Adolescent in Family Therapy: A Developmental and Narrative Approach (1999)*. She has written numerous scholarly articles and has presented nationally and internationally on several topics including technology, infertility, family dinners, couple therapy, reflecting teams, and parenting issues across the life cycle. She is an editor for the *Harvard Review of Psychiatry* and for *Couple and Family Psychology: Research and Practice*.

Dr. Fishel is a founding member of The Family Dinner Project, a nonprofit group that helps families online and in communities to have better and more frequent family dinners. She writes about parenting issues and lectures widely to parent and teacher groups. She has also written articles about family issues for NPR, PBS, Psychology Today, *The Washington Post*, and other media outlets.

Dr. Fishel maintains a private practice in psychotherapy with adults, couples, and families, and lives outside Boston with her husband.

Index

TITLES FROM OUR PSYCHOLOGY COLLECTION

Anthony Chambers and Corinne Datchi, Editors

Justice in Life and Society: How We Decide What is Fair
by Virginia Murphy-Berman

A Guide for Statistics in the Behavioral Sciences
by Jeff Foster

College Student Psychological Adjustment: Exploring Relational Dynamics that Predict Success
by Jonathan F. Mattanah

Perfectionism in School: When Achievement Is Not so Perfect
by Kathryn L. Fletcher and Kristie L. Speirs Neumeister

Children with Emotional and Behavioral Disorders: Systemic Practice
by Marianne Celano

Momentum Press is one of the leading book publishers in the field of engineering, mathematics, health, and applied sciences. Momentum Press offers over 30 collections, including Aerospace, Biomedical, Civil, Environmental, Nanomaterials, Geotechnical, and many others.

Momentum Press is actively seeking collection editors as well as authors. For more information about becoming an MP author or collection editor, please visit http://www.momentumpress.net/contact

Announcing Digital Content Crafted by Librarians

Momentum Press offers digital content as authoritative treatments of advanced engineering topics by leaders in their field. Hosted on ebrary, MP provides practitioners, researchers, faculty, and students in engineering, science, and industry with innovative electronic content in sensors and controls engineering, advanced energy engineering, manufacturing, and materials science.

Momentum Press offers library-friendly terms:

- perpetual access for a one-time fee
- no subscriptions or access fees required
- unlimited concurrent usage permitted
- downloadable PDFs provided
- free MARC records included
- free trials

The **Momentum Press** digital library is very affordable, with no obligation to buy in future years.

For more information, please visit **www.momentumpress.net/library** or to set up a trial in the US, please contact **mpsales@globalepress.com**.

www.ingramcontent.com/pod-product-compliance
Lightning Source LLC
Chambersburg PA
CBHW070730220326
41598CB00024BA/3371